W9-BLO-487

Yemen

Yemen

BY LIZ SONNEBORN

Enchantment of the World
Second Series

Children's Press®

A Division of Scholastic Inc.

NEW YORK   TORONTO   LONDON   AUCKLAND   SYDNEY
MEXICO CITY   NEW DELHI   HONG KONG
DANBURY, CONNECTICUT

Frontispiece: The town of al-Mahwit

Consultant: Janet C. E. Watson, Professor of Arabic, University of Salford, United Kingdom

Please note: All statistics are as up-to-date as possible at the time of publication.

Book production by Herman Adler

Library of Congress Cataloging-in-Publication Data

Sonneborn, Liz.
 Yemen / By Liz Sonneborn.
   p. cm.—(Enchantment of the world)
 Includes bibliographical references and index.
 ISBN-13: 978-0-516-25296-4
 ISBN-10: 0-516-25296-8
 1. Yemen (Republic)—Juvenile literature. I. Title. II. Series.
 DS247.Y48S65 2007
 953.3—dc22   2007012202

SCHOLASTIC, CHILDREN'S PRESS, and associated logos are trademarks and/or registered trademarks of Scholastic Inc.
1 2 3 4 5 6 7 8 9 10 R 17 16 15 14 13 12 11 10 09 08   08

Yemen

Contents

Cover photo:
A Yemeni girl

The landscape
near Abyan

A woman wearing
traditional jewelry

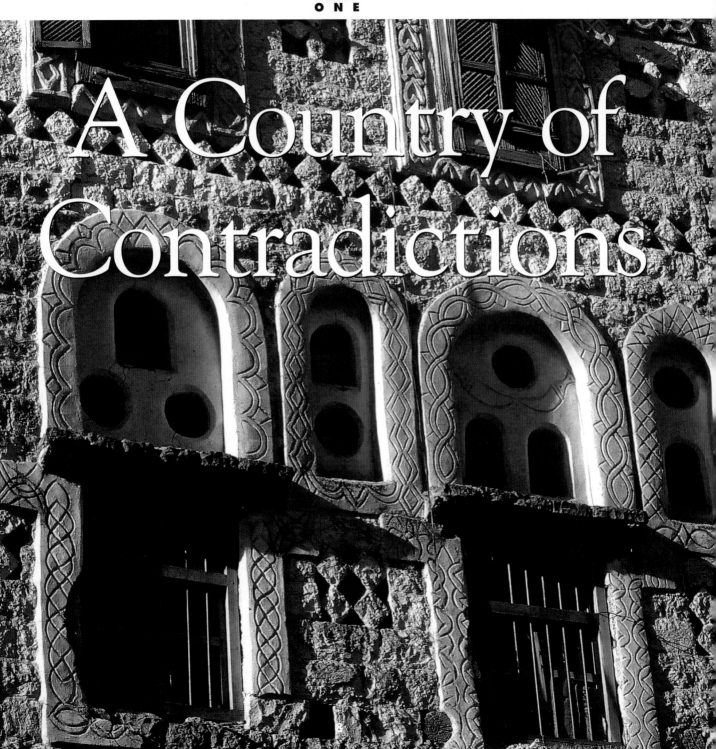

A Country of Contradictions

THREE THOUSAND YEARS AGO, A BEAUTIFUL HOOPOE BIRD flew to the great King Solomon of Israel. The king knew the language of birds, and the hoopoe had an important message for him. The bird explained that he had been in the land of Sheba, which was ruled by a woman living in a fabulous palace. The hoopoe told King Solomon that the people of Sheba worshipped the Sun rather than God.

Solomon wrote a letter to the queen and gave it to the hoopoe to deliver. He instructed the bird to watch the queen's reaction to what he had written. When the queen opened the letter, she found a stern request from Solomon that she visit him and join those who followed the one true God.

Fearing that Solomon might invade her realm, the queen decided to send the king a gift. But Solomon was not impressed. He told the hoopoe that any gift from the queen could not compare with the blessings he had already received from God.

The queen then decided to meet with Solomon. She journeyed to his palace, which was made of glass. After speaking with the king, she repented her sun worship and agreed to worship God.

Opposite: **Sanaa is famous for its unique architecture.**

Solomon and the Queen of Sheba, **a painting by Frans Francken the Younger (1581–1642)**

The story of this ancient queen appears in the Qur'an, the holy book of the religion of Islam. A slightly different tale appears in the Bible. According to the biblical story, King Solomon's wisdom was famous far and wide. The queen of Sheba heard about it and went to Jerusalem to test him. Impressed by his wisdom, she paid him in gold, spices, and precious stones. The king, in turn, was taken with his guest and gave her gifts in return.

For centuries, people have been fascinated by the tale of the Queen of Sheba. No less intriguing is the story of Yemen, the country that sits on the southern tip of the Arabian Peninsula in what was once the ancient land of Sheba.

This ornate copy of the Qur'an dates to the 1600s. Both the Qur'an and the Bible include stories of King Solomon and the Queen of Sheba.

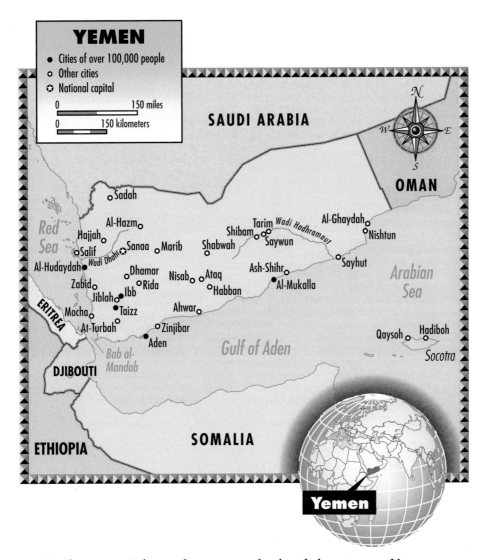

As the queen's legend suggests, the land that is now Yemen was once home to an early civilization. Sheba, or Saba, as it is sometimes known, was one of the most prosperous places on the globe. More recently, however, Yemen has not enjoyed the level of prosperity that its earlier civilization experienced. Through the ages, the Yemenis have fought foreign invaders and too often battled among themselves. This ongoing history of war and civil war has severly hurt the Yemeni economy.

Thousands of ancient buildings crowd the historic center of Sanaa. Many are decorated with white gypsum.

In 1990, the Yemenis tried to end the strife by coming together to create a unified nation, the Republic of Yemen. But the scars of Yemen's troubled past had left their mark. A jewel of the ancient world, Yemen is now one of the poorest nations in the Arab world.

This is just one way Yemen is a country of contradictions. Its landscape is also a study in contrasts. Like most of the Arabian Peninsula, much of Yemen is a vast desert. But Yemen's highlands offer green valleys and cool breezes, and its coastal areas are renowned for their beautiful beaches.

Its settlements are likewise varied. Many Yemenis live in small villages. But a growing number are moving to large cities, such as Sanaa and Aden. There, modern steel-and-glass skyscrapers often stand blocks away from dwellings made of mud bricks that were built many centuries ago.

The Yemenis embrace a mixture of old and new in their daily lives. Some work as farmers, using traditional methods to till their fields. Others work in new industries, such as oil refining and concrete manufacturing. Many observe traditional customs while also adopting modern ways. They might recite ancient Yemeni poetry one night and watch television the next.

The very character of the Yemeni people is itself an unexpected mix. They have endured many years of war, poverty, and social upheaval. Yet they are known as lively and fun-loving. Yemenis are famed for their keen sense of humor and unshakable spirit of generosity. Even as they deal with the legacy of their difficult past, they remain full of hope.

A Yemeni man uses an ox to plow his field. More than half of Yemenis work in agriculture.

The Green Land of Arabia

A surprising number of trees survive in Yemen's rocky landscape.

IN THE MIDDLE EAST, THE PART OF THE WORLD WHERE ASIA and Africa meet, there is a large peninsula called Arabia. This peninsula is home to many oil-rich countries, including Saudi Arabia, Oman, Kuwait, and the United Arab Emirates. These nations lie in the great Arabian Desert, a land that is largely hot, dry, and barren.

At the southern tip of the Arabian Peninsula sits Yemen. Unlike its neighbors, it has only limited oil resources, but it is blessed with a rich and varied landscape. There are beautiful coastal areas with amazing coral reefs. There are high mountain retreats with cool and crisp air all year-round. And there are lush green valleys covered with fruit trees and grapevines. Because of these lovely landscapes, Yemen has earned the nickname "the Green Land of Arabia."

Opposite: **The Hanish Islands lie off Yemen's west coast. Adventurous travelers dive among the teeming fish and other creatures that live in the nearby shallow waters.**

Yemen's Geographic Features

Area: 203,850 square miles (527,968 sq km)

Lowest Elevation: Sea level, along the coast

Highest Elevation: 12,336 feet (3,760 m), at Jabal an-Nabi Shu'ayb

Largest Island: Socotra, 1,409 square miles (3,650 sq km)

Largest City: Sanaa, 1,653,300 people

Highest Average Temperature: June, 80°F (27°C)

Lowest Average Temperature: January, 57°F (14°C)

Highest Annual Rainfall: In the highlands, 8 to 30 inches (20 to 76 cm)

Lowest Annual Rainfall: On the coast, 3 to 9 inches (7 to 22 cm)

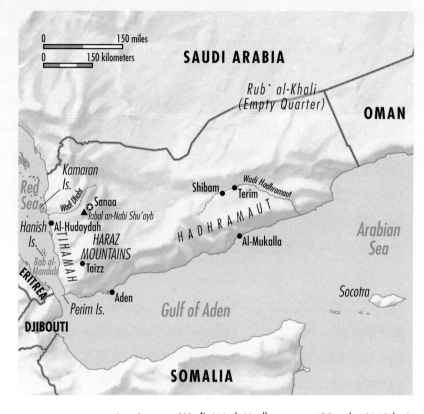

Longest Wadi: Wadi Hadhramaut, 400 miles (640 km)

Longest Border: With Saudi Arabia, 906 miles (1,458 km)

> ### Locating Yemen

Yemen is the forty-ninth largest nation in the world, slightly smaller than France and about double the size of the state of Wyoming. Yemen borders two other Middle Eastern nations— Saudi Arabia to the north and Oman to the east. To the south of Yemen lies the Gulf of Aden and the Arabian Sea. To the west lies the Red Sea. At the country's southwestern tip is the

The Gate of Tears

Bab al-Mandab is Arabic for "Gate of Tears." It's a fitting name for the strait that separates Asia from Africa. Over the centuries, many sailors have died while trying to navigate this narrow waterway.

A legend provides a second explanation for the strait's name. According to the legend, before Bab al-Mandab was formed during a deadly earthquake that tore apart the continents of Asia and Africa.

strait known as Bab al-Mandab. This waterway, which measures only about 17 miles (27 kilometers) across at its narrowest point, connects the Gulf of Aden and the Red Sea. It is one of the most active shipping areas in the world. Across the Bab al-Mandab are the African countries of Eritrea and Djibouti.

A view of Africa and Asia from space. The two continents nearly touch at the Bab al-Mandab.

The Island of Socotra

Socotra is the largest of Yemen's many islands. Its name, which comes from the ancient Sanskrit language, means "Island of Bliss." To visitors, even Yemenis from the mainland, it seems a strange world. Until recently, Socotra was largely isolated. Its people developed their own unique culture. Their language, Soqotri, is completely different from the Arabic spoken in the rest of the country. Speakers of Yemeni Arabic cannot understand it.

Many people on Socotra are farmers or herders who earn their living just as their ancestors did. Generally, their homes have no running water or electricity. At one time, the island was accessible only by boat. It was completely cut off from the rest of the world between June and September, when frequent storms and winds made the journey by boat impossible.

Then, in 1999, the Yemeni government opened the first paved airstrip on Socotra, so jets could land there. Now, people travel from the mainland to the island year-round.

The airstrip is just one step the government has taken to develop the island. Yemen is also trying to attract tourists to Socotra. Many travelers from Europe and North America are drawn to the magnificent coral reefs off its coast. Scuba divers off Socotra can also get a close look at sea turtles and other creatures.

The government of Yemen controls more than one hundred islands in the waters off its mainland. Many are small and uninhabited, while the larger ones are home to thousands of people. The biggest Yemeni island is Socotra, which is located in the Arabian Sea. Also notable are Kamaran and the Hanish Islands in the Red Sea and Perim in the Bab al-Mandab.

Bir Ali beach on the Arabian Sea is considered one of the most beautiful beaches in all of Yemen.

The Coastal Plains

Yemen's mainland is divided into three zones—the coastal plains, the highlands, and the desert.

The coastal plains are a flat, narrow strip of land that runs along the Red Sea and the Gulf of Aden. The area on the Red Sea coast is known as the Tihamah, meaning "Hot Lands." This region is generally hot and humid. Even in winter, the average temperature is about 89 degrees Fahrenheit (32 degrees Celsius). In summer, it averages 104°F (40°C).

The Green Land of Arabia **19**

Between May and October, frequent dust storms make the coast even more uncomfortable. High winds gusting from the Red Sea blow up dust, silt, and sand. The flying particles can make the air so dark that no sunlight shines through. Often, airports have to shut down because planes cannot take off with so much dirt clogging their engines.

The coast gets very little rain. On average, it sees only about 9 inches (23 centimeters) of rainfall a year. It rains far more in the highlands. Some of this water flows down to the coast, but it quickly evaporates in the heat of the Tihamah. Stores of mountain water remain beneath the ground, however. By pumping this water to the surface for irrigation, Yemenis can farm in the dry coastal region.

The Highlands

Just inland from the coastal plains along the Red Sea are the western highlands, which run from Yemen into Saudi Arabia. Here, the land is dominated by flat-topped hills. Located on a plateau in the western highlands is Sanaa, Yemen's capital and largest city.

The area is also home to great mountains, including Jabal an-Nabi Shu'ayb, which rises 12,336 feet (3,760 meters). This stunning peak is the highest point not just in Yemen, but in all of the Arabian Peninsula. Because of its mountains, Yemen is sometimes called "the Roof of Arabia."

The central highlands lie farther to the east, parallel to the Gulf of Aden. This area, too, is mountainous, although its peaks and plateaus are generally lower than those of the western highlands.

The highlands enjoy the most temperate climate on the Arabian Peninsula. Average temperatures range from 71°F (22°C) in June to 57°F (14°C) in January. Temperatures sometimes soar during the day and plunge at night. During winter, temperatures may even fall below freezing. When the weather turns bitter cold, the Yemenis of the highlands put on warm jackets made from sheepskin.

The rocky Haraz Mountains rise in western Yemen. Tiny villages perch atop some peaks.

Looking at Yemeni Cities

Sanaa, the nation's capital, is the largest city in Yemen. Second in size is Aden (right). Located on the Gulf of Aden, it is the country's busiest port. The city has a long history as a merchant town. As a center of trade, Aden attracted the attention of foreign invaders, including the British, who ruled the city from 1839 to 1963. Now a modern city of about 510,400 people, Aden retains much of its historical character. Its oldest section is located in the crater of an extinct volcano.

Yemen's third-largest city is Taizz (left), with a population of about 406,900. Located in the fertile highlands, it has a mild climate, with warm days and cool nights. Its economy is largely based on farming. Coffee is its most important crop. The city is also known for its cotton, jewelry, and cheese.

Al-Hudaydah lies along the Red Sea in western Yemen. It is the nation's fourth-largest city, with a population of about 382,400. In 1961, it suffered a major fire, but it was built up again in the following decades. Once largely a fishing town, Al-Hudaydah is now filled with concrete buildings and asphalt roads. It is Yemen's second-largest port.

The village of Manakha is nestled high in the Haraz Mountains. Terraces were cut into the steep slopes hundreds of years ago.

Capturing the Rain

The highlands are the wettest region of Yemen. The rainy seasons are April through May and July through August. At these times, monsoon winds blow from the sea into the mountains, bringing moisture. The rainfalls are unpredictable, coming in short, intense spurts. Sometimes, they result in flash floods, which can destroy villages.

These rains are welcomed by the people of the highlands. Farmers build complicated irrigation systems that collect rainwater and carry it to mountain slopes. These slopes are cut into steps, called terraces, that create flat fields on which to grow vegetables, fruit trees, and grains.

The seasonal rains also collect into long valleys called *wadis*. Generally, Yemen is so dry that it has no permanent lakes or rivers. But during the rainy season, wadis become temporary riverbeds. This allows the surrounding lands to be farmed.

The Wadi Hadhramaut

The most fertile area of all is the Wadi Hadhramaut region of central Yemen. After the rains, it becomes green with vegetation. The region is especially famous for its date trees. Despite its fertility, the craggy landscape of the Wadi Hadhramaut is forbidding. Its name is said to come from an Arabic phrase meaning "death is present."

The Hadhramaut region is home to two especially striking towns. Shibam, which is about two thousand years old, is surrounded by a great wall. Within the walls are hundreds of multistory houses made of mud bricks. Some of these houses date back to the sixteenth century. The pattern they make against the sky is reminiscent of a modern city skyline. For this reason, Shibam is nicknamed "the Manhattan of the Desert."

Another ancient town, Tarim, is known for its many mosques. Mosques are places of worship for Muslims, people who practice the religion of Islam. Tarim has 365 mosques, one for each day of the year.

Date trees dot the valley floor in Wadi Hadhramaut.

The Desert

The northern edge of the Hadhramaut region slopes down into a vast stretch of sand. The area, which is part of the Arabian Desert, is known as the Rubʻ al-Khali, meaning "the Empty Quarter." This desert region makes up about half of Yemen.

The Empty Quarter lives up to its name. Unlike the rest of Yemen, it is largely barren. The area receives almost no rainfall. In fact, many years can pass without a single drop of rain falling there.

The Empty Quarter has few people or permanent settlements. Those who do live there are mostly Bedouin tribespeople. The Bedouin herd camels and other animals, traveling from place to place in search of grazing areas for their livestock. While Yemenis elsewhere are increasingly embracing modern ways, the Bedouin of the Empty Quarter live much as their ancestors did hundreds of years ago.

Many Bedouins in the Empty Quarter live in tents. The Bedouins can quickly take apart the tents and move to a new place.

Wondrous Life

YEMEN IS A LAND OF VARIED TERRAINS AND CLIMATES. NOT surprisingly, the plants and animals found in the country also vary from region to region.

The desert supports little life. Few plants can survive in an area so dry. Animals are also rare. Flies and mosquitoes buzz through the air, while poisonous scorpions scurry along the sandy ground.

Opposite: **The south Arabian leopard is the largest cat in the Arabian Peninsula.**

Scorpions come out at night to hunt. They eat insects, spiders, and other small creatures.

Living things also have a hard time in the hot, humid coastal areas. The region supports relatively few native animals and only sparse patches of wild vegetation. Some farmers, however, tap the water beneath the ground to grow crops.

In the highlands, however, a wide array of plants and animals can be found. From tall trees to colorful flowers, from mighty baboons to delicate butterflies, thousands of species thrive in this part of Yemen.

Male baboons are almost twice as large as female baboons. They have gray hair that falls over their shoulders.

Dragon's Blood

The island of Socotra is full of strange and beautiful plant life. One famous example is the dragon's blood tree. The tree, which is a member of the lily family, looks rather odd. Fanning out from its trunk are thick branches with tufts of leaves at the end. This gives it a weird mushroomlike shape that would look at home in a Dr. Seuss illustration.

When the bark of the dragon's blood tree is cut, a deep red resin oozes out, giving the tree its name. Yemenis have found many uses for the resin. It makes an excellent dye. People have also used it as a medicine to treat a variety of problems, from stomach ailments to headaches to eye diseases.

The ancient Roman writer Pliny heard a legend explaining the origin of dragon's blood. In Pliny's version, elephants and dragons were once at war with each other. One day, a dragon attacked an elephant by snaking its tail around the giant animal's back legs. As the dragon had hoped, the elephant fell down, but his heavy body landed on the dragon. Both were injured, the warm blood of the elephant mingling with the cold blood of the dragon. This created the hard resin of the dragon's blood tree.

The Date Palm

Dates are a favorite food throughout the Middle East. These delicious and nutritious fruits come from the date palm tree. Date palms flourish in the Wadi Hadhramaut. The date palm has deep roots, which can tap into water stored underground. Yemeni date palms can grow more than 90 feet (27 m) tall and thrive for decades. The oldest live for 150 years. Besides providing food, date palms are also cut for timber, and their leaves are woven inte furniture and baskets.

Acacia trees are common in Yemen. They produce clusters of bright flowers after a rain.

Many kinds of fruit, including bananas, mangoes, oranges, and limes, grow well in Yemen.

Plants in the Highlands

Yemen's highlands are home to more than six hundred species of flowering plants. They include tamarisk, ficus, and acacia. Yemenis use the small yellow and white flowers of the acacia bush to make dyes.

Trees also yield a variety of delicious fruits and nuts. Mango and papaya trees grow in the western highlands. Almond, peach, and apricot trees are common in the central highlands.

Hyenas have powerful jaws. They can crush and chew up bone.

From Gazelles to Geckos

Most of Yemen has few animals. Only the mountainous area is different. The wild creatures that live there include gazelles, leopards, mountain hares, and hyenas. The Arabian wolf and several species of foxes also make the region their home.

The gelada baboon is one of the largest animals in Yemen. These majestic beasts can be seen crawling up and down rock faces in the mountains. Hamadryas baboons also live in Yemen. Some Yemenis adopt these animals as pets.

In the Wadi Hadhramaut, it is common for women to wear tall straw hats while herding goats.

Most Yemeni farmers raise livestock, especially cattle, for meat and milk. Many families also keep sheep, goats, or chickens.

Camels can be found in eastern Yemen. But for an Arab country, Yemen has relatively few camels. Many Yemenis live in cities and villages. They do not need camels to haul their possessions through the desert as many less-settled peoples do.

More than 360 species of birds fly in the skies above Yemen. Many are migratory, passing through on their way to somewhere else. In the highlands, ravens and vultures are common. Other birds found in Yemen include hawks, parrots, buzzards, honeysuckers, and weaver finches.

Bearded vultures pick up the bones of dead animals with their feet. They drop the bones on rocks from great heights to crack them open, exposing the nutritious marrow inside.

Small lizards, such as geckos and chameleons, are common in most of Yemen. In rocky areas, cobras, vipers, and other snakes frequently slither about. Yemen is also home to more than three thousand types of insects, including about one hundred species of butterflies.

Locusts fly into Yemen from Africa. These pests are a menace to farmers. A swarm of locusts can quickly destroy an entire field of crops. Yemenis have found one good use for locusts. They roast the insects to make a tasty treat!

Veiled chameleons spend much of their time in trees. They get most of the water they need by licking the dew from leaves.

Socotra's Natural Wonders

The plants and animals on the island of Socotra are amazingly varied and unusual. Hundreds of plant and animal species are unique to Socotra and nearby islands. They are found nowhere else in the world. These include the bottle tree (left), the Socotra sunbird, the Socotra leaf-toed gecko, and the only member of the cucumber family that grows into a tree.

Protecting Yemen's Wildlife

In recent years, many plants and animals in Yemen have become endangered. As the human population has grown, more and more land has been cleared to make way for homes and other buildings. As a result, much of the habitat of animals, such as the South Arabian leopard, has been destroyed. Some animals, including several species of gazelles, have already become extinct.

Goats graze on the meager grasses in the Wadi Hadhramaut. Overgrazing is a growing problem, as the number of goats in Yemen doubled between 1996 and 2005.

Another problem is that Yemenis sometimes allow livestock to overgraze. Some areas where native grasses once grew have been stripped completely bare. Without these grasses to hold the fertile topsoil in place, powerful winds blow it away, leaving once-rich farmland barren.

With some Yemeni plants and animals facing extinction, Yemen's government is making efforts to better manage its land and resources. Only time will tell whether these measures will be enough to save the country's most threatened species.

Saving the Marine Turtle

Yemen is home to five of the world's seven species of marine turtles. Its beaches are important nesting areas for species such as green turtles and leatherback turtles. But the survival of these large swimming turtles is now in question.

Yemen's marine turtles face a number of threats. People often harvest the turtles' eggs before they have a chance to hatch. Beachfront development disrupts their natural nesting areas, so the turtles lay fewer eggs in the first place. In addition, many young turtles are killed before they are old enough to reproduce. They fall prey to polluted water or fishing nets. Conservationists want to protect nesting areas and encourage fishers to adopt turtle-friendly fishing methods.

If marine turtles disappeared, Yemen's economy would suffer. Tourism is fast becoming a major industry. Many tourists flock to Yemen just for the chance to go turtle watching off the coast.

From Ancient to Modern

YEMEN IS HOME TO ONE OF THE MOST ANCIENT CULTURES in the world. Many Yemenis believe that the area that is now northern Yemen was first populated by the ancestors of the biblical figure Shem. One of Noah's sons, Shem is considered the first of the Semites, the ancient people from whom both Arabs and Jews are descended. The Bible states that his people founded a city called Azal. Yemenis now often identify Azal as Sanaa, their country's capital city.

Opposite: **The historic city of Marib was the capital of the ancient Sabean kingdom.**

Parts of the ancient Sabean Temple of Bilqis date back to the seventh century B.C.

History records that by about 1000 B.C., southern Arabia was home to several kingdoms. The most powerful was Saba, also known as Sheba. These kingdoms grew up along overland trade routes, over which caravans of camels hauled treasured trade goods. These goods included luxury items, such as silk from China, spices and woven cloth from India, and ivory from Africa. But perhaps the most prized goods of all

From Ancient to Modern **39**

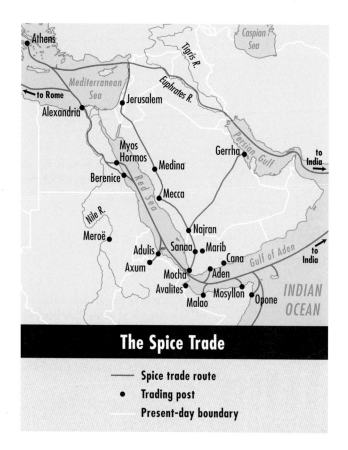

The Spice Trade

— Spice trade route
● Trading post
— Present-day boundary

were frankincense and myrrh, which are produced from the resin of certain trees that grow along the coast of southern Arabia.

Frankincense and myrrh were burned as incense during religious rituals. Myrrh was also used in medicines, perfumes, and makeup. Both substances were treasured by many ancient peoples, including the Egyptians, the Greeks, and the Romans. According to the Bible, the three wise men who visited the Christ child brought gifts of frankincense, myrrh, and gold from Saba.

The Sabean Kingdom

The incense trade made Saba wealthy. The population of its capital, Marib, which is in the western highlands, grew to almost three hundred thousand. To feed the people of Marib, in about 500 B.C. the Sabeans built a great dam. This dam would create a lake during the rainy season. With this water, the Sabeans were able to irrigate about 4,000 acres (1,600 hectares) of farmland.

Saba's dominance in the region was eventually challenged by other kingdoms, including Qataban and Hadhramaut. By about A.D. 300, a tribal people called the Himyarites had become the most powerful force in the region.

Marib

The small city of Marib is an archaeological marvel. It was once the capital of the kingdom of Saba. Today, it contains some of the country's most spectacular ancient ruins. These include portions of ancient buildings with Sabaean inscriptions on their walls. Visitors to Marib can also see several tall pillars (left), the only remains of the Temple of Bilqis. Archaeologists believe that the temple was built nearly three thousand years ago. Near Marib are the ruins of the great dam built there around 500 B.C. Measuring about 2,000 feet (600 m) across, the dam remained standing for a thousand years.

Southern Arabia proved vulnerable to foreigners. In about A.D. 525, Ethiopians, a people from Africa, overran the Himyarite lands. Fifty years later, the Himyarites—with the help of the Persians, who came from the area east of Arabia that is now Iran—drove out these invaders. The Persians, however, refused to leave, so the Himyarites remained under the control of foreigners.

By this time, the incense trade had become less lucrative for the Himyarites. A safe sea route between India in South Asia and Egypt in North Africa had been discovered, making it easier to transport goods by ship than overland. The market for frankincense and myrrh was drying up. The Christian faith was spreading through the region, and Christians did not use frankincense and myrrh in their ceremonies.

Ghumdan

Legend holds that the rulers of Saba built a palace called Ghumdan. It supposedly rose twenty stories high. On the roof were bronze sculptures of lions and eagles. It was said that when the wind blew, these sculptures roared and shrieked. The roof itself was covered with a layer of alabaster, a beautiful white stone. It was so thin that people inside could look up and watch the birds flying overhead. In the tenth century, a poet and historian named Abu Muhammad al-Hasan ibn Ahmad al-Hamdani wrote of Ghumdan:

> It rises, climbing into the midst of the sky,
> Twenty floors of no mean height,
> Wound with a turban of white cloud
> And girded with alabaster.

The Prophet's Message

In the seventh century, a new religion began in Arabia—one that would have an enormous impact on the people of Yemen. Beginning in about 610, a prophet named Muhammad is said to have received revelations from God, whom Arabs call Allah. He started to preach God's word, telling his followers that there was only one true God. At the time, most people in Arabia believed in many gods. Within a few years, Muhammad gained converts to his religion, which was called Islam. Its followers are called Muslims.

One early convert to Islam was the Persian governor in southern Arabia. He became a Muslim in 628 and insisted that those he ruled follow suit. At about this time, people started calling the region Yemen, which means "the Right Side" in Arabic. The name referred to the side of the Arabian Peninsula where Yemen is located. It was the "right" side because that side is closer to the holy city of Mecca, where Muhammad was born.

In the centuries that followed, a line of competing Muslim rulers controlled Yemen. The most significant belonged to the

Zaydi sect. In the late seventh century, Muslims had split into two groups—Sunnis and Shi'is. The Zaydis were the descendants of Zayd ibn Ali Zayn al-Abidin, a Shi'i leader and the great-great-grandson of Muhammad. The Zaydis called their leaders *imams*. From the late ninth century on, the Zaydi imams had great influence over northern Yemen.

Queen Arwa

For more than fifty years, southern Arabia was ruled by Queen Arwa (1048–1138), a member of the Sulayhid dynasty. She married her first cousin, Ahmad al-Mukarram al-Sulayhi, in 1066. The next year, he became ruler but was too ill for the job. It fell to Queen Arwa to lead her people. After her husband's death, she married his cousin, which allowed her to continue her reign. After he died in 1101, she ruled alone until her own death. Queen Arwa was renowned for her charity. She was also a learned woman. Chroniclers wrote of her vast knowledge of poetry, science, and the Qur'an, the holy book of Islam.

During her reign, Queen Arwa decided to move Yemen's capital from Sanaa to the city of Jiblah. There, she built the Palace of Al-Mu'ez. The grand structure included 365 rooms. Queen Arwa supposedly slept in a different one each night of the year, so would-be assassins would not know where to find her.

Queen Arwa also had a great mosque constructed in Jiblah (left), where she was buried in 1138. Much of the original building still stands today. This architectural wonder attracts many tourists.

Foreign Control

Various groups had long struggled for power in Yemen. But starting in the 1500s, the region was overrun with foreigners from distant lands. They were trying to control the shipping routes between the Mediterranean region and the Far East. The first to get a foothold in Yemen were the Portuguese. In 1513, they seized the island of Socotra and made an unsuccessful attempt to take over Aden.

The Portuguese actions alarmed the Turks of the Ottoman Empire, who themselves wanted more influence over Yemen. By 1548, the Turks had conquered not only Aden but also the cities of Taizz and Sanaa. Under the Turks, Yemen's trade with Europe flourished. Coffee became one of their most important exports. Grown in the Yemeni highlands, coffee beans bound for Europe were shipped out of the port city of Mocha on the Red Sea.

The Zaydis finally drove the Turks out of Yemen in 1636. Although the Turks still had some control over coastal areas, the Zaydis were the greatest influence in the highlands to the north.

Dividing Yemen

Wanting its own foothold in Yemen, Britain established a coaling station in Aden. British ships on the way to India stopped there to refuel. The relationship between the Yemenis and the British was fairly good until 1839, when robbers attacked an Indian ship sailing under the British flag. The British used the attack as an excuse to send two warships into Aden, seize the city, and declare it a British colony.

Under British control, Aden thrived as a commercial center. To protect it from the Turks, the British worked with local leaders outside the city. In this way, the British extended their influence over much of southern Yemen, which became known as the Aden Protectorate.

In the mid-nineteenth century, the Turks made a bid to restore their control over Yemen. In the north, they regained authority in the Tihamah region in 1849 and expanded eastward toward the cities of Taizz and Saada. Like the British, the Turks were looking to control trade in Yemen, which became even more important after the opening of the Suez Canal in 1869. This waterway connects the Red

People lined the banks of the Suez Canal on the day it opened in 1869. It had taken eleven years to build.

Sea and the Mediterranean Sea. Using the Suez Canal, ships could travel between Europe and Asia without having to sail around Africa.

Not surprisingly, the Turks and the British often clashed over who controlled what part of Yemen. In 1905, the two countries agreed on a border, dividing the region in two. The British controlled South Yemen, while North Yemen fell under the control of the Turkish Ottoman Empire.

The Rule of Imam Yahya

The Turks in North Yemen faced opposition from the Yemenis. There were constant uprisings. But then the Turks were defeated in World War I. With their empire in ruins, they were no longer powerful enough to remain in North Yemen. In 1920, they officially ended their rule in the region.

After the Turks left, a Zaydi imam named Yahya bin Muhammad Hamid al-Din became the most powerful leader in North Yemen. Using force, he brought the lands of local political rivals under his control. Yahya wanted to extend his rule into South Yemen but decided his forces could not take on the British army. He also feared Saudi Arabia, which briefly went to war with Yemen in 1934.

Colonial Yemen, 1914

British territory	Italian territory
French territory	Ottoman territory
Independent	Present-day Yemen

The same year, Yahya signed an agreement with the British to avoid future conflict.

To further secure his control over North Yemen, Yahya tried to isolate the country from outside influences. People were allowed only the most limited contact with foreigners. He also worked to make North Yemen economically self-sufficient, so it would not have to rely on foreign aid.

The Palace of the Rock

One of the most unusual buildings in Yemen lies on the outskirts of Sanaa. Dar al-Hajar, or the Palace of the Rock, is five stories high. It was built by Imam Yahya as his summer home in the 1930s. The palace sits atop a high rock that towers over the fertile valley of Wadi Dhahr. Dar al-Hajar is so popular in Yemen that it has almost become a symbol of the country. Just as Americans look at the Statue of Liberty and think "United States," Yemenis see Dar al-Hajar and think "Yemen."

Some Yemenis strongly opposed Yahya's rule. They included a group called al-Ahrar al-Yamaniyyin, meaning "the Free Yemenis." The group wanted reforms that would help modernize the country. The Free Yemenis staged a revolt in 1948. They assassinated Yahya and tried to take over the government. Brutal fighting then broke out between the Free Yemenis and a group led by Yahya's son Ahmad. Ahmad's followers quickly drove his rivals out of the country, and he became North Yemen's new leader.

Yemeni Jews look at a map of the newly created Jewish state of Israel in 1948. Many Jews left Yemen for Israel at this time.

In 1962, Colonel Abdullah al-Sallal was serving as bodyguard to Muhammad al-Badr, the leader of North Yemen. Al-Sallal would soon take over the government and become president of the new Yemen Arab Republic.

Creating the Yemen Arab Republic

To keep control, Ahmad ruled with an iron fist. He treated his political opponents brutally and many Yemenis lived in fear. In 1955, army officers, with the help of Ahmad's brother Abdullah, plotted to take over the government. Once Ahmad discovered the plan, he had Abdullah killed.

Ahmad ruled until his death in 1962. His son Muhammad al-Badr became the new ruler. Less than a week later, however, he fled into the mountains when army officers seized control of the government. They announced that their country would now be called the Yemen Arab Republic (YAR). Colonel Abdullah al-Sallal became the new nation's president.

In the meantime, al-Badr formed his own army and began to fight back. The country was now in civil war. Several foreign nations got involved. Britain and Saudi Arabia supported al-Badr's followers, who were called the royalists. Egypt and the Soviet Union (a large nation composed of Russia and other now-independent countries in eastern Europe and southern Asia) backed al-Sallal's supporters, who were called the republicans. Because of the foreigners' help, both sides were armed with modern weapons. They waged a long fight that destroyed villages and killed many thousands of soldiers and civilians.

After years of fighting, the republicans were dealt a serious blow when Egypt, engulfed in political and military troubles of its own, withdrew its troops from the YAR in 1967. The royalists took the opportunity to surround Sanaa, but in the end, the republicans held them off. By 1970, the republicans had emerged as the clear winner.

Trouble in the South

During the bloody conflict in the north, South Yemen was also in turmoil. Various groups had risen up against the British. The fighting even reached the streets of Aden, plunging the city into chaos.

By 1967, the rebels had come together to establish the National Liberation Front (NLF). Deciding they could not defeat the determined NLF, the British withdrew their troops from South Yemen. On November 30, the NLF declared southern Yemen an independent country—the People's Republic of South Yemen. The name would be changed three years later to the People's Democratic Republic of Yemen, or PDRY.

From the beginning, the country struggled to survive. The war and declining trade in Aden left the region's economy in shambles. The government demanded financial compensation from Britain for its long occupation, but the British offered only a token payment.

Two Yemens

In 1970, there were officially two Yemens—the YAR in the north and the PDRY in the south. Both nations were having such economic troubles that they had to rely on aid from foreign powers. The YAR received money from Saudi Arabia and Britain, while the PDRY took aid from the Soviet Union.

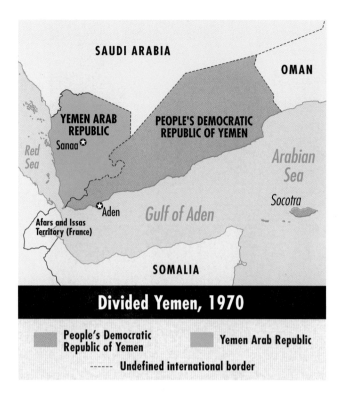

Divided Yemen, 1970

People's Democratic Republic of Yemen

Yemen Arab Republic

------ Undefined international border

As early as 1972, the two governments discussed coming together to create a unified Yemen. But their political and economic philosophies were very different. The PDRY was a communist country, in which the government controlled all business and industry. By the late 1970s, the YAR had embraced capitalism, the economic principle that guides the United States and many other Western countries. Under capitalism, businesses are privately owned and far more independent of government control. Military skirmishes at the border added to the tension between the countries. With this gulf between the two Yemens, talks of unification stalled.

Economic conditions in the YAR began to improve under Ali Abdullah Saleh, who became president in 1978. In the south, though, the PDRY continued to struggle. Fighting between rival political factions resulted in a brief but bloody civil war there in 1986. In the late 1980s, the PDRY also

Ali Abdullah Saleh became president of the Yemen Arab Republic in 1978. When the two Yemens united in 1990, he became president of the new Republic of Yemen.

suffered due to a drop in aid from the Soviet Union, which was itself nearing economic collapse and would break apart in 1991.

Coming Together

In this atmosphere, the idea that the two Yemens might do better by uniting into one finally took hold. In 1988, the two governments again began talking about unification. And on May 22, 1990, the dream of one Yemen became a reality. On that day, the Republic of Yemen was born. Its president was Ali Abdullah Saleh, the former president of the YAR. The vice president was Ali Salim al-Baydh, a noted politician from the PDRY.

The new republic wanted to maintain peace by giving power to officials from both the north and the south. But this tore the new country apart. In 1994, a faction supporting the president and a faction supporting the vice president went to war with each other. Saleh's followers triumphed in this brief civil war.

Throughout its long history, Yemen has frequently been a bed of conflict. It battled a host of foreigners and endured violent infighting while Yemenis struggled among themselves for control. But at the beginning of the twenty-first century, Yemen at last seems on the dawn of a new age, one in which all its peoples could come together to mend their frayed nation.

Yemen and Terrorism

On the morning of October 12, 2000, the USS *Cole* sailed into the Yemeni port of Aden. The American ship was scheduled to stay there a few hours to refuel. While it was anchoring, an explosion blew an enormous hole in the *Cole*'s hull. Seventeen American servicemen were killed.

The *Cole* had been the target of two suicide bombers, who approached the ship on a rubber boat. Within days, American investigators discovered who was behind the attack. It was al-Qaeda, the terrorist network led by Osama bin Laden. The next year, al-Qaeda would be responsible for the September 11 attacks on New York City and Washington, D.C.

After the attack on the *Cole*, Yemeni president Ali Abdullah Saleh pledged that his country would work with the United States in fighting terrorism. Saleh had learned a valuable lesson after the Gulf War (1991). During that conflict, Yemen had supported Iraq in its war against the United States and its allies. This endangered Yemen's ability to get the foreign aid it needed. For the rest of the 1990s, Saleh had to scramble to rebuild relations with Western nations and its powerful Middle Eastern neighbors, such as Saudi Arabia.

Although the Yemeni government says it is working to combat terrorism, it has not always been successful. In 2002, a French tanker called the *Limburg* was bombed off the coast of Yemen. And in 2006, thirteen al-Qaeda members, including those involved in the *Cole* and *Limburg* attacks, escaped with ten other prisoners from a Yemeni jail.

Governing Yemen

YEMEN'S CONSTITUTION DIVIDES THE NATIONAL GOVERN-ment into three branches—the executive, the legislative, and the judicial.

Opposite: **Ali Abdullah Saleh is the only president the Republic of Yemen has ever had.**

The Executive Branch

At the top of the executive branch is the president, who serves as head of state and commander-in-chief of the nation's military. The president serves a seven-year term.

Since 1999, the president has been elected by popular vote. Anyone over age eighteen can vote. According to the constitution, there must be at least two candidates, both of whom need the endorsement of the parliament, the nation's lawmaking body.

The 301 members of Yemen's House of Representatives are elected to six-year terms.

A Pioneering Woman

Among Yemeni women, Amat al-Aleem Alsoswa stands out for her many "firsts." She was the first woman to be a popular television announcer in Yemen. She was the nation's first female ambassador, representing Yemen in Sweden, Denmark, and the Netherlands. And in 2003, Alsoswa became the first woman in Yemen's Council of Ministers. As the minister of human rights, she advised President Ali Abdullah Saleh about policies involving violations of the basic rights of Yemeni citizens, such as the right to a fair trial and the right to free speech. She was also concerned with discrimination against women, which continues to be a problem in Yemen. In 2006, Alsoswa began working as the director of the United Nations Development Programme's Bureau for Arab States.

Alsoswa credits her mother with making her own success possible. Although her mother could not read or write, she pushed Alsoswa to get a good education. She eventually earned degrees from Cairo University in Egypt and American University in Washington, D.C. Alsoswa returned home to pursue a career, first in journalism and then in politics. As minister of human rights, she worked to improve her country's human rights record. In her words, "The opening up Yemen has undergone since 1990 has made it logical for us to create this ministry. The whole country is becoming more progressive."

The head of government is the prime minister, who is chosen by the president. The president also has a Council of Ministers who provide advice in various areas. For instance, there are ministers of defense, education, culture, finance, and human rights. These ministers are appointed by the president with input from the prime minister.

The parliament is the lawmaking body in the Yemeni government. Since 2001, it has been made up of two separate houses—the Shura Council and the House of Representatives.

The Shura Council consists of 111 people, who are selected by the president. The House of Representatives has 301 members. They are elected by the people to six-year terms. Most representatives elected in 2003 were from the General People's Congress, the most powerful political party in Yemen.

In addition to enacting laws, the parliament is responsible for overseeing government spending and approving international treaties.

NATIONAL GOVERNMENT OF YEMEN

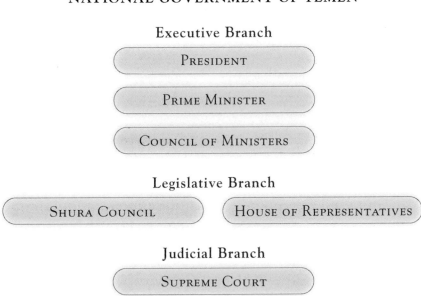

Executive Branch

PRESIDENT

PRIME MINISTER

COUNCIL OF MINISTERS

Legislative Branch

SHURA COUNCIL

HOUSE OF REPRESENTATIVES

Judicial Branch

SUPREME COURT

The third branch of Yemen's government is the judiciary. The nation's highest court is the Supreme Court.

The legal code of Yemen is based on Islamic law. As a result, it must conform to the laws of Islam known as the *shar'ia*, meaning "God's way." Shar'ia is based on the Qur'an and the Hadith, which is a book of sayings and deeds by the Prophet Muhammad that were collected by his followers after his death. Judges in Yemen have to be religious scholars so that they can properly evaluate whether laws and punishments are in keeping with the rules set forth in shar'ia.

A judge questions a witness in court.

Governorates are responsible for education in Yemen. Many schools are badly underfunded, especially in rural areas.

Local Government

The country of Yemen is divided into nineteen divisions, called governorates, or *muhafazat*. (The city of Sanaa is officially called a municipality, but it functions much like a twentieth governorate.) Each governorate is headed by a local official, called a governor.

The governorates are further divided into districts. In each district, a local council deals with important issues. For instance, these councils are responsible for addressing local health concerns, overseeing education, and collecting taxes in their districts.

The National Flag

When Yemen became a unified nation in 1990, it adopted its national flag. The flag features three horizontal stripes—red, white, and black. The same colors are found on the flags of other Middle Eastern countries, including Egypt, Syria, and Iraq. The red stripe symbolizes the bloodshed during Yemen's battles for independence, the white stripe stands for the hope the Yemenis have for the future, and the black stripe recalls the nation's troubled history.

Each district also has its own court, which deals with both criminal and civil cases. If a party to a lawsuit disagrees with the verdict of a district court, it can take its case to a court of appeal, administered by the governorate. A court of appeal decision can in turn be appealed to the Supreme Court in Sanaa.

Government in Action

The constitution of Yemen sets forth the duties and responsibilities of the different government bodies. But these requirements have not always been followed to the letter. In fact, the country's political landscape in recent years has reflected an old Yemeni proverb: "Ruling Yemen is like trying to dance on the head of a snake."

Since unification, the primary "dancer" in Yemeni politics has been Ali Abdullah Saleh. On May 22, 1990, the same day the governments of northern and southern Yemen decided to come together to form a single nation, Saleh was chosen as the new country's president.

Charming and charismatic, Saleh took on the daunting task of trying to bring together all the people of Yemen. Under his leadership, unified Yemen survived the 1994 civil war. All the while, Saleh voiced his commitment to making Yemen a thriving democracy.

Yemeni women hold up their voting cards as they wait in line to vote in the 2006 presidential election.

The First Elections

In 1999, the first year Yemenis could vote for their president, they were given little choice in whom to vote for. Two main political parties had emerged in Yemen—the General People's Congress (Saleh's party) and the Islah Party. Convinced it could not get the votes needed to win, the Islah Party decided not to run a candidate that year. Saleh then arranged for another member of his own party to run against him, in a show of obeying the constitutional rule requiring two candidates. Not surprisingly, Saleh won in a landslide, receiving more than 96 percent of the vote.

The 2006 presidential election was far more dramatic. Saleh announced that he was not going to run. His party then held a series of rallies in which his supporters

Supporters of President Ali Abdullah Saleh hold up posters of him during a rally. The election of 2006 was the first time Saleh faced a real challenger since coming to power in 1978.

The National Anthem

The national anthem of Yemen is titled "United Republic." It was originally the national anthem of South Yemen and became the official anthem of the Republic of Yemen after unification.

Repeat, O World, my song.
Echo it over and over again.
Remember, through my joy, each martyr.
Clothe him with the shining mantles
Of our festival.
Repeat, O World, my song.
In faith and love I am part of mankind.
An Arab I am in all my life.
My heart beats in tune with Yemen.
No foreigner shall dominate over Yemen.

begged him to change his mind. Finally, Saleh, still seemingly reluctant, agreed to enter the campaign. Many people believed he had staged the events to make himself look like a humble servant of the people.

Saleh was in less control over what happened next. To his surprise, five different opposition parties came together to support another candidate, Faisal bin Shamlan. Both campaigns immediately turned vicious, with each slinging mud at the other. Bin Shamlan's side accused Saleh of corruption, while Saleh's side suggested bin Shamlan wanted to start

The Only President

Ali Abdullah Saleh has served as the president of the Republic of Yemen since it was founded in 1990. He was born in 1942 in the village of Bayt al-Ahmar near Sanaa. At sixteen, he joined the armed forces of Imam Ahmad, the ruler of northern Yemen. In 1962, he was wounded during the revolt that overthrew the imams and established the Yemen Arab Republic (YAR).

Saleh rose in the ranks, becoming an officer in the YAR army. In 1978, the nation's president was murdered, and its parliament elected Saleh to succeed him. As president of the YAR, Saleh focused on improving the country's economy and pushing for its unification with the People's Democratic Republic of Yemen, or PDRY. In 1988, under his leadership, the YAR became the first country in Arabia to have a parliament whose members were chosen by popular election.

When the two Yemens were unified, Saleh became the president of the new republic. Saleh's administration

weathered a civil war in 1994 and has since worked to maintain stability and foster economic growth.

another civil war. The race was so heated that on election day, television newcasters made a point of reminding voters not to take guns to their polling places.

In the end, Saleh was reelected, but this time he received only 77 percent of the vote, suggesting his lock on power might not be as absolute as his followers had previously believed. The election also showed that Yemeni politics remain unpredictable and complex. For Yemen's leaders, the dangerous dance on the head of a snake is likely to continue.

Sanaa: Did You Know This?

"Sanaa must be seen, even if the journey is long." This old saying shows the pride Yemenis have in their largest city. Nestled on a flat plain in the western highlands, Sanaa is one of the oldest cities in Arabia. It has been inhabited for more than 2,500 years.

Until the 1960s, most of the city was contained within a clay wall standing 20 to 30 feet (6 to 9 m) high. In fact, the name Sanaa means "Fortified Place." It was possibly used as a fortress by the ancient Sabeans.

Within the old walled portion of the city are more than one hundred mosques and six thousand houses. All were built before the eleventh century. In recent years, preservationists have been working to keep the oldest buildings intact.

As the capital of Yemen, Sanaa is also home to many grand government buildings. Among them are the president's residence and the parliament building.

In recent decades, Sanaa has grown quickly, doubling in population almost every four years. In 2005, the number of people living in Sanaa was an estimated 1,653,300. To accommodate its exploding population, the city has spilled beyond the old walls. Sanaa now struggles with big-city problems, such as poor sanitation and a lack of drinking water. Like Yemen as a whole, it is an intriguing mixture of the old and the new.

U.S. Embassy

Sanaa University

City Wall

OLD TOWN

Al-Bakiliyah Mosque

Qat Souq

National Museum

Salah ad Din Mosque

Fortress

Prime Minister's Residence

Souq al-Milh (market)

Yemeni Parliament

Military Museum

Jami al-Kabir Mosque (Great Mosque)

French Embassy

Ministry of Tourism and Environment

British Embassy

Ethiopian Embassy

Canadian Consulate

Dutch Embassy

Saudi Arabian Embassy

U.A.E. Embassy

Presidential Palace

0   1,000 meters
0   1,000 yards

Sanaa

Earning a Living

66

Although Yemen has made progress in recent years, it remains the poorest Arab nation. In fact, it is one of the poorest countries in the world. More than 45 percent of Yemenis live in poverty. In 2006, an estimated eight million Yemenis were living on the equivalent of less than US$2 a day.

Yemen's geography is partly to blame for its economic woes. The low rainfall in most of Yemen makes it difficult to farm. And the oil reserves under Yemen's desert lands are much smaller than those in other Arab countries such as Kuwait and Saudi Arabia.

Opposite: **Fishing is important to Yemen's economy. Most fish caught off Yemen's shores are sold in local markets.**

Despite the development of Yemen's oil industry in recent years, the nation's poverty rate has not improved since the two Yemens united in 1990.

A History of Economic Troubles

Yemen's troubled history has also hurt its economy. The decades before unification produced particularly tough economic times.

In northern Yemen, the imams who ruled before 1962 purposely isolated the region. By keeping out foreign influences, they also prevented their people from developing modern industries. Later, after the Yemen Arab Republic was founded, the disruptions of civil war and a drought that made farming impossible only added to northern Yemen's problems.

Yemeni farmers plant onions. Most Yemenis work in agriculture.

In southern Yemen, the communist economic policies of the government of the People's Democratic Republic of Yemen proved disastrous. Also, the Suez Canal, which connects the Red Sea and the Mediterranean Sea, was closed from 1967 to 1975. This reduced trade in Aden, the region's most important commercial center. As a result, the government had to rely on aid from foreign allies, especially the Soviet Union. But as the Soviet Union headed toward collapse, this aid dried up, leaving southern Yemen in dire straits.

These economic troubles prompted the two Yemens to unite. Each came to believe that together they had a better chance of building a prosperous nation. But this was not going to be easy.

The Suez Canal cuts across Egypt for more than 100 miles (160 km).

An American tank rolls across the Saudi Arabian desert during the Gulf War. Yemen's position on the war brought it into conflict with its Middle East neighbors and with world powers like the United States.

One economic problem the country faced resulted from the Gulf War (1991). During this conflict, an international force headed by the United States went to war with Iraq after Iraq had invaded Kuwait. Yemen opposed the use of force against Iraq. To punish Yemen for its stance, Saudi Arabia, a U.S. ally, forced between half a million and a million Yemenis who were working in Saudi Arabia to leave the country. These Yemenis, mostly men, had been working in Saudi Arabia's oil industry.

This flood of men back into Yemen was a big economic blow to the young country. Suddenly, the nation had to cope with legions of unemployed men. Meanwhile, the men's families fell into poverty.

Even more devastating was the 1994 civil war. Though President Ali Abdullah Saleh's army quickly defeated the rebel forces, the upheaval stalled all economic growth.

After the civil war, President Saleh sought financial help from other countries. In the years since, Yemen has received billions of dollars in loans and grants from international organizations. These include the International Monetary Fund, the World Bank, and the United Nations. In November 2006, Yemen secured a promise of US$4.6 billion in aid from the World Bank.

Many Yemeni men continue to work in foreign countries. They send a portion of what they make back to family members in Yemen. Often, their family's very survival depends on this money.

Yemeni Money

The basic unit of currency in Yemen is called the *rial*. Coins come in values of 1, 5, and 10 rials. Paper money has values of 20, 50, 100, 200, 500, and 1,000 rials. In 2007, US$1 equaled about 198 rials.

The images on the paper money celebrate the beauty and heritage of Yemen's greatest cities. A picture of the port of Aden is on the 20-rial bill. The 50-rial bill shows the historic town of Shibam, and on the 100-rial bill is the capital city of Sanaa.

Most Yemenis working abroad live in nearby Arab countries. But more distant nations also have large Yemeni immigrant communities. They include Indonesia, India, the United Kingdom, and the United States.

Living off the Land

Back at home, most Yemenis earn a living the way their ancestors did—by farming fields and raising animals. About 60 percent of Yemenis work in agriculture. But little of the land is fertile, so the average farmer cannot grow much and thus earns little for his or her labor. Despite the large number of farmers in Yemen, agriculture accounts for only about 12 percent of the annual gross domestic product, the total value of all goods produced in the country.

Only about 3 percent of Yemen's land is used for farming. Since the country receives little rain, most fields need to be irrigated for crops to grow.

The most fertile areas in Yemen are the highlands, the Tihamah coastal plain, and the Hadhramaut region. In the highlands, fields are built on terraces, which prevent the rich topsoil from being washed away in sudden downpours or blown away by strong winds. On the coastal plain, the land is irrigated from water trapped below the ground. In the Hadhramaut region, the great Wadi Hadhramaut catches rainwater, which farmers then redirect to their fields.

Yemenis grow a wide variety of fruits and vegetables, including tomatoes, grapes, mangoes, apricots, radishes, leeks, and onions. Their farms also produce many types of grains. The most popular is sorghum, but farmers also grow wheat, barley, and millet. Yemenis also grow tobacco and cotton.

Many rural families raise animals. They sometimes keep cows for milk and meat. Sheep and goats, often tended by children, provide milk, wool, and hides. Some Yemenis also raise chickens for their eggs and meat.

Children herd goats in the mountains near Sanaa. There are an estimated 7.3 million goats in Yemen.

Coffee is made from the berries of the coffee plant. The berries are peeled, cleaned, roasted, and ground before they are used.

Coffee and Qat

Historically, coffee was one of Yemen's most important agricultural exports. For two hundred years, most of the coffee Europeans drank came from Yemen. Much of it was shipped from the port of Mocha, a word that in English came to mean certain kinds of coffee.

Increasingly, Yemenis have replaced the coffee in their fields with qat. This shrub produces leaves that, when chewed, release a stimulant similar to coffee's caffeine. In the past, only the wealthy chewed qat. But now, many Yemenis chew qat with their friends in the afternoon.

Demand for qat is so high that many farmers have stopped growing other crops. Yemen now imports most of its food from other countries. Another problem with qat cultivation is the amount of groundwater it uses. Though qat does not need as much water as other crops, farmers often water it more than needed in order to make it grow more quickly. In some areas where qat is grown, many wells will likely run dry in the near future.

But qat's main problem is its cost to families. Poor Yemenis who spend much of their income on qat have to do without other goods.

What Yemen Grows, Makes, and Mines

Agriculture (2000)

Sorghum	401,000 metric tons
Tomatoes	245,000 metric tons
Sheep	4,760,000 head

Manufacturing

Cement (2001)	1,493,000 metric tons
Gasoline (2001)	1,081,000 metric tons
Wheat flour (2000)	338,000 metric tons

Mining

Oil (2003)	21,400,000 metric tons
Salt (1998)	147,000 metric tons
Gypsum (1999)	103,000 metric tons

Working in Industry

In recent years, many Yemenis have moved to cities in the hopes of making a better living than farming offers. Some work in factories. Among the goods manufactured in Yemen are processed foods, soft drinks, cigarettes, and housewares. The manufacture of tiles, bricks, cement, and other building materials is also important to the economy. As more workers move to cities, these materials are needed to construct homes and workplaces.

Even with a demand for manufactured goods, operating factories in Yemen is often difficult. In many areas, supplies of electricity and water are unreliable. And many roads are unpaved, making it hard to transport goods and workers.

Some Yemenis make their living in the fishing industry. The Red and Arabian seas are teeming with mackerel, squid,

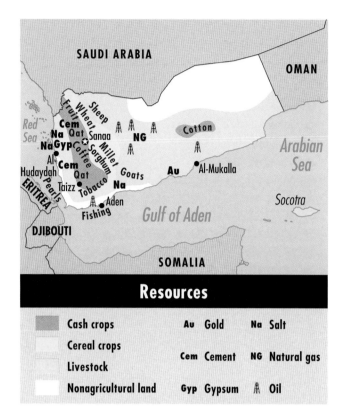

Resources

	Cash crops	Au	Gold	Na	Salt
	Cereal crops				
	Livestock	Cem	Cement	NG	Natural gas
	Nonagricultural land	Gyp	Gypsum	Å	Oil

shrimp, tuna, and lobster. Most fishers work for themselves. There are not enough fish-processing plants in Yemen to make it a big business.

Wealth from Oil

The most important industry in Yemen is oil refining. Modest oil reserves were first found in Yemen in the 1980s. Ever since, the government has been working to make the most of this resource.

In 2005, the country exported about US$3 billion worth of oil. This money accounted for about 70 percent of the government's total revenue. Yemen's government is also making plans to export its untapped reserves of natural gas.

The bonanza of oil money is not likely to last long, however. Yemen's oil reserves are expected to be tapped out by 2015, if not sooner.

An Adventure Destination

In the late 1990s, as Yemen became more politically stable, the government began developing a new industry—tourism. One great obstacle in this effort has been kidnappings. In several cases, tribal groups have taken foreign tourists hostage in an effort to pressure the government to address their complaints.

Nevertheless, the government has had success encouraging foreign investors to build new hotels, restaurants, and convention centers. Larger cities, such as Sanaa and Aden, offer travelers luxury hotels. But most tourists from North America and Europe are looking to take advantage of the relatively low cost of vacationing in Yemen. For instance, an American can easily tour the country spending only US$15 a day.

Tourists come from all over the world to see the remnants of Yemen's ancient cultures. The Marib Dam, which dates back 2,500 years, was one of the first dams ever built.

Many tourists come to Yemen to see historical attractions, such as the old section of Sanaa and the archaeological sites at Marib. But Yemen is also increasingly popular with more adventurous travelers. Travel reporter Tom Downey explains, "New outfits offer grueling treks to mountaintop villages, four-wheel-drive safaris through untrammeled deserts and sailing voyages aboard ancient dhows to isolated . . . islands." Scuba divers are particularly drawn to the island of Socotra, with its largely untouched beaches and offshore coral reefs.

The Yemeni People

Large families are typical in Yemen.

YEMEN IS THE MOST DENSELY POPULATED COUNTRY ON THE Arabian Peninsula. In 2006, the number of Yemenis was estimated at 21,456,188. In recent years, the country's population has grown quickly, and experts believe it could rise even faster in the years to come. Yemen has one of the highest birthrates in the world. The average Yemeni woman has six children. Some predict the population could double by the year 2030.

Not surprisingly, Yemen has a very young population. Nearly half the people are fifteen years old or younger. Largely because of poor health care, only about 2.6 percent of Yemenis are older than sixty-five.

Opposite: **Yemen has one of the youngest populations of any country in the world. Its median age is sixteen, meaning that the same number of Yemenis are under sixteen as are over sixteen.**

Most Yemenis are of Arab descent. Others trace their origins to East Africa.

Ethnic Yemen	
Arab	91.7%
Afro-Arab	6.3%
Other	2.0%

An Arab Nation

Ethnically, nearly all Yemenis are Arabs. Most of the non-Arabs are immigrants from Africa and Europe. Some Arab Yemenis living in the Tihamah coastal plain are also of African descent. With only the narrow Red Sea separating the Tihamah from the African continent, coastal Yemenis and nearby African populations have often been in contact with one another.

Social Rank

Traditionally in Yemen, people's ancestry determined their place in society. Whether they were born into the highest social rank or the lowest, they were likely to stay there for the rest of their lives. In modern Yemen, education has given people more social-class mobility. But the old social traditions still have a big impact on the opportunities open to many Yemenis.

At the top of the Yemeni social ladder are the Sayyids. They are considered the direct descendants of the Prophet Muhammad. In the past, the Sayyids were often government officials and landlords. Today, they are often highly regarded healers and teachers. Qadis are also well-respected in Yemen society. They are revered as scholars of Islamic law.

A teacher with his students. More than 80 percent of Yemeni boys attend school.

Below these elite groups are the tribal peoples of Yemen. Tribes are led by sheiks, wise men who are called upon to settle disputes among the people of their village. Tribes living in different areas have different customs. Each has its own style of dressing, favorite foods, and type of dances and celebrations. Yemenis can identify a man's tribe just by looking at the way he wraps his turban around his head.

Generally, tribal peoples are more devoted to their tribe and their sheik than to the country as a whole. Tribes are

Turbans are commonly worn by men throughout Yemen.

A Bedouin family relaxes after a meal. The canvas fence protects them from the wind.

often suspicious and even hostile to government officials who try to exert authority over them. As a result, one of the greatest challenges for the modern Yemeni government is winning the continued support of sheiks and the people who follow them.

Most tribal people in Yemen live in settled villages. The exception are the Bedouins, who make up about 1 percent of the Yemeni population. Traditionally, these desert people were animal herders. They lived as nomads, constantly traveling from place to place. In recent years, some Bedouins have left this way of life to work in the oil industry.

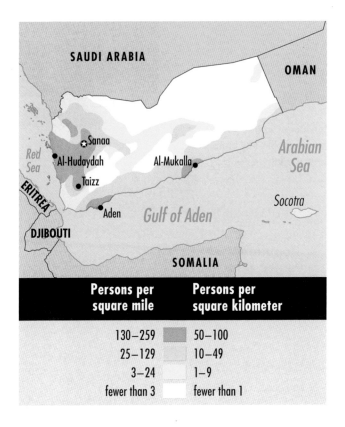

Persons per square mile		Persons per square kilometer	
130–259		50–100	
25–129		10–49	
3–24		1–9	
fewer than 3		fewer than 1	

In villages in the wadis, many people live in mud-brick buildings.

Population of Major Yemeni Cities (2005)	
Sanaa	1,653,300
Aden	510,400
Taizz	406,900
Al-Hudaydah	382,400
Al-Mukalla	156,800

Urban and Rural

How Yemenis live depends a great deal on where they live. Most Yemenis are rural people. About three-quarters of the population live in small villages. The rest are city dwellers. As Yemen's industries grow, however, more and more people are likely to move to urban areas, where they can generally make a better living.

Most of the Sayyids, Qadis, and other elite groups live in Yemen's cities. City dwellers also include workers in the manufacturing and service industries. Many urban Yemenis look down on rural people for their lack of sophistication and ignorance of modern ways.

People in rural areas have their own prejudices against city dwellers. They say cities are unhealthy, and living there makes people frail and sickly.

In Sanaa, modern buildings are common outside the historic center.

The Arabic Language

For all their differences, most Yemenis are united by their language. The vast majority speak Arabic. Most people in Yemen learn classical Arabic. This ancient version of Arabic is the language of the Qur'an. People use classical Arabic when reciting passages from this holy book. In day-to-day life, however, Yemenis generally use a more modern version of Arabic. In school, children learn to read and write Modern Standard Arabic. At home, they speak one of the many dialects, or variations, of Yemeni Arabic.

Writing in Arabic

The Arabic language is written using the Arabic alphabet, which has twenty-eight characters. Words are written from right to left. Often, one letter will run into the next, creating a beautiful design as well as a readable text.

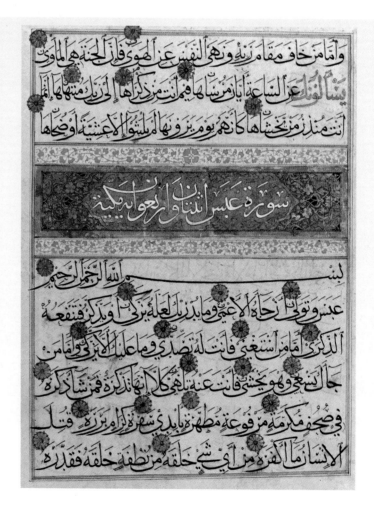

Some students in Yemen also study a second language. English is the most popular foreign language, although French is often offered in private schools. A few Yemenis in the south know Russian because of the region's past relationship with the Soviet Union. Some African languages are spoken by African immigrants in Yemen.

A small number of native Yemenis are not Arabic speakers. Among these are people who live on the island of Socotra. Geographically and culturally isolated from the rest of Yemen, the people on Socotra speak Soqotri, which is related to the language spoken in the ancient kingdom of Saba. Soqotri and Arabic are so different that Yemenis from Socotra cannot hold a conversation with people from the mainland. In the Mahra governorate, in eastern Yemen, many people speak the Mehri language.

More than two hundred million people around the world speak Arabic. It is the primary language of the Middle East and North Africa.

Bathari

Very few of Yemenis speak the Bathari language. It is used in just two countries—Yemen and Oman. Only about two hundred people today know how to speak Bathari.

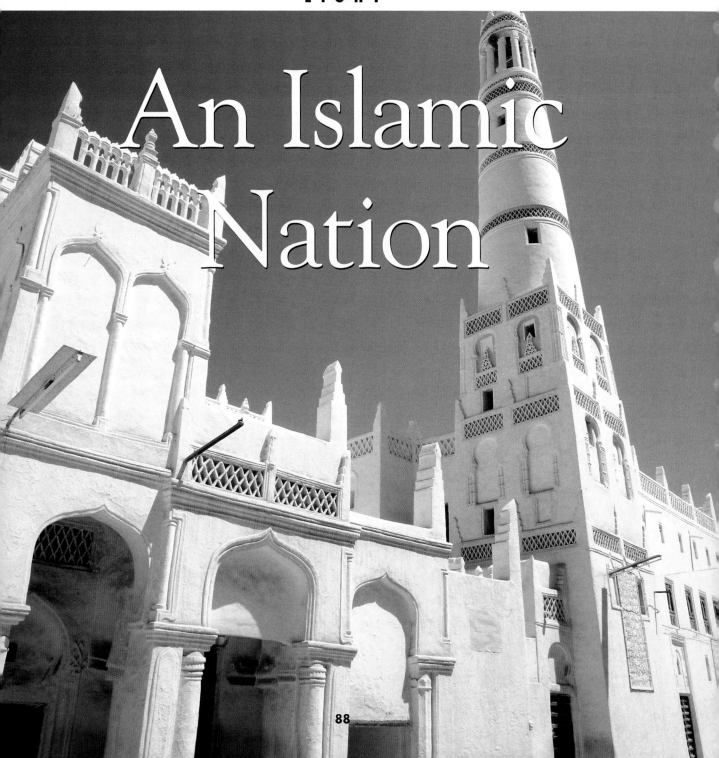

An Islamic Nation

ALMOST ALL THE PEOPLE OF YEMEN HAVE ONE THING in common. Nearly 99 percent of them are followers of Islam. Most of the remaining 1 percent are Hindus, Christians, and Jews. Many of these people are from other countries. They live in Yemen to do business or to go to school.

Islam is central to life in Yemen. It is the country's official religion, and non-Muslims are not allowed to hold elected office. The legal system also recognizes Islam as the source of all laws.

Opposite: **Yemen is home to thousands of mosques.**

In Yemen, all work stops when it is time to pray.

Religion in Yemen

Islam	98.9%
Hinduism	0.7%
Christianity	0.2%
Other	0.2%

The Great Prophet

Islam came to Yemen more than 1,350 years ago. In 628, the Persian governor who then ruled the region converted to Islam. He insisted that his subjects become Muslims as well.

Only about twenty years earlier, Muhammad, the great Prophet of Islam, had begun preaching this new religion. Muhammad was born in 570 in the city of Mecca in what is now Saudi Arabia. A traveling merchant, Muhammad had a religious experience when he was about forty years old. Muslims believe he was visited by the angel Gabriel. For the next twenty years, the angel told Muhammad the word of God, whom Muslims call Allah.

In Mecca, Muhammad began to tell others of God's messages. He tried to persuade them to abandon the many gods they worshipped and instead turn to Allah. Muhammad also urged them to live their lives according to the commands revealed to him by Gabriel. Muhammad quickly attracted followers, who wrote down the messages he had received. These were compiled into the Qur'an, the sacred book of Islam. They also collected Muhammad's sayings about how a proper Muslim should behave in a book known as the Hadith.

As Muhammad's following grew, the authorities in Mecca became suspicious of him. Fearing for his life, Muhammad fled Mecca and headed north to the city of Medina in 622. The Prophet's trek from Mecca to Medina became known as the Hijra. Muhammad continued to attract converts to Islam. When Muhammad died in 632, most Arabs had already become Muslims.

Abu Bakr ibn Abdullah al-Aydarus

In the city of Aden, Abu Bakr ibn Abdullah al-Aydarus (1447–1508/09) is remembered as a great holy man. Al-Aydarus grew up in the Hadhramaut region, where he received his early religious education. After moving to Aden, al-Aydarus became famous for having amazing powers.

One story holds that he magically prevented a ship from sinking. As the ship started going down, he went into a trance and then hurled a stick at a mountaintop. The stick popped the peak off the mountain, which fell precisely into the hole in the ship, stopping the flow of water and saving the vessel and its crew. Another legend says that al-Aydarus saved the people of Aden from a famine by making milk fall like rain from the sky. Aden now shows its gratitude to al-Aydarus by holding an annual festival in his honor.

Sunni and Shi'i

Following the Prophet's death, two factions emerged among the Muslim peoples. One faction was the Sunnis. They believed that the caliph (Muhammad's successor) should be elected by a group of elites. The other faction was the Shi'is. They believed that the caliph should be directly descended from Muhammad.

Today, the estimated 1.2 billion Muslims in the world still divide themselves into Sunnis and Shi'is. The Sunnis are the larger of the two groups. About 85 percent of the world's Muslims are Sunni.

About two-thirds of Yemenis are Sunni and one-third are Shi'i. Most people in the south and southeast are Sunni, while most in the north and northwest are Shi'i. In the cities, many neighborhoods house a mixture of the two groups.

Islam's two major groups are subdivided into smaller sects. Yemeni Sunnis belong to the Shafi'i sect. Most Shi'i in Yemen belong to the Zaydi sect. Zaydis have long had a powerful

A man reads from the Qur'an, Islam's sacred book. Almost all Muslims memorize at least part of the Qur'an.

influence over the culture and politics in the northern highlands. A minority of Yemen's Shi'is belong to the Ismaili sect.

The Five Pillars

Muslims in Yemen, and around the world, accept certain religious duties that are known as the Five Pillars of Islam. The first pillar is the *Shahadah*. It requires Muslims to affirm their faith by stating, "There is no God but God, and Muhammad is his Prophet." The second pillar is *Salah*, which obliges Muslims to pray five times a day. The third, *Zakat*, requires believers to give money to the needy. The fourth, *Sawm*, calls on them to fast for religious purposes. And the fifth, *Hajj*, commands that Muslims who can afford it travel to the holy city of Mecca at least once during their life.

Pilgrims to Mecca visit the city's Great Mosque to pray at the Kaaba. This black cube-shaped building is the most sacred shrine in Islam.

The Jews of Yemen

Jewish people lived in Yemen from before the time of Muhammad. For many centuries after Islam spread across the Arabian Peninsula, Jews were the largest non-Muslim group in Yemen. During the time of the Zaydi imams, a vibrant Jewish community thrived in northern Yemen. Many Jews made their living as merchants. They were also renowned as craftspeople. At one time, about half of the people in the city of Sanaa were Jewish.

In 1948, the Jewish state of Israel was established. Tired of living as a minority in an Arab country, most Yemeni Jews decided to move to Israel. Now, only a few hundred Jews still live in Yemen.

Daily Prayers

Of the Five Pillars, Salah has the most obvious effect on everyday life in Yemen. In fact, people's entire days are structured around their daily prayers.

Before sunrise, Yemenis offer their prayers. Men often go to the local mosque, while women and children generally pray at home. Everyone then goes about their daily routine.

When the Sun is high in the sky, Yemenis stop what they are doing to offer their midday prayers. When they are done, it is time for lunch. In the afternoon, they pray for the third time. After the afternoon prayer, men gather together to socialize and chew qat.

After sunset, people pray again. Families then come together for their evening meal. Afterward they relax together, perhaps talking or watching television, until it's time for the fifth prayer of the day. Everyone then goes off to bed, ready to wake the next day and start the cycle again.

Islamic tradition requires that daily prayers be performed in a specific way. Muslims bow and kneel, often on special prayer rugs, and recite portions of the Qur'an. They touch their heads

The Call to Worship

Mosques feature high towers called minarets. Traditionally, when it was time for prayer, an official known as a *muezzin* climbed to the top and loudly called out, telling everyone to stop and pray. In modern mosques, the muezzin usually makes the call to prayer using a microphone and loudspeakers.

to the floor to indicate their total submission to God. When praying, they always face in the direction of Mecca.

For their prayers to be meaningful, Muslims must be in a state of mental and physical purity. As part of the purification process, they must wash their hands, face, arms, and feet. In parts of Yemen where water is scarce, people may cleanse themselves with sand or make the movements of the washing ritual with dry hands.

Religious Festivals

The ninth month of the Islamic calendar is called Ramadan. Muslim tradition holds that during this month, Muhammad received his first messages from the angel Gabriel. For Muslims, it is the holiest time of the year. In accordance with Sawm, the fourth pillar of Islam, all Muslims—except for the very young, the very old, and the sick—must fast during the daylight hours throughout Ramadan. They eat a morning meal before dawn (called *suhoor*) and an evening meal after sunset (known as *iftar*).

During Ramadan, Yemeni Muslims are also expected to take extra time for religious observance. Some visit mosques more often or make a special effort to read and study

The Islamic Calendar

To determine when to celebrate religious holidays, Muslims consult the Islamic calendar. This calendar is based on the the Moon's movements. It includes twelve months and 354 days—11 days less than the 365-day Western calendar used in much of the world. As a result, the dates when Muslim holy days are celebrated change from year to year. Ramadan begins on September 2 in 2008, and on August 22 in 2009.

the Qur'an. People also try to spend time with their friends and family.

After Ramadan, Yemenis celebrate the breaking of their month-long fast with the three-day festival of 'Id al-Fitr. During this time, people exchange gifts with their loved ones, and everyone enjoys an array of tasty foods. Children dress in new clothes and light firecrackers as part of the fun.

Yemenis also observe 'Id al-Adha. This festival commemorates the willingness of the prophet Ibrahim (known as Abraham in the Bible) to sacrifice his son for God. On this day, Muslims often kill an animal for a feast served to family and friends. Other religious holidays celebrated by Yemenis mark the day that Muhammad was born and the day he rose into heaven.

Sparks fly from a traditional cannon as Yemenis celebrate the end of Ramadan.

Poetry
and Other
Pleasures

Music and dance are central to Yemeni life.

In Yemen, art is a vital part of everyday life. At afternoon get-togethers, Yemenis play music and recite poetry. During celebrations, friends and family gather to dance and sing. Yemen's artistic traditions are also evident in the beautiful objects they make, from their delicate jewelry and colorfully woven cloths to the ornate daggers Yemenis proudly wear at their waists.

Opposite: **The city of Tarim is famous for its elaborate mud-brick palaces.**

Mosques are the most notable buildings in many Yemeni cities. Minarets tower over the surrounding landscape.

Perhaps the Yemenis' most impressive art is their homes and mosques. The people of Yemen are proud of their houses. Often, they celebrate the construction of a house by painting the date it was completed on the front in decorative writing.

The style of housing differs depending on what natural resources are available for building materials in a region. In the coastal areas, for example, Yemenis build simple, low-lying houses out of reeds. In the desert town of Shibam, people construct multistory buildings out of sun-dried mud bricks. And in the highlands, houses are likely to be constructed from brick and stone.

The Tower House

Perhaps the most famous housing style in Yemen is the tower house. Some six thousand tower houses stand in the old section of Sanaa. Portions of many of these houses are more than one thousand years old.

Most tower houses have five to eight stories. The ground floor is for storage. The next few floors are used as living areas. The top floor includes the house's most beautiful room—the *mafraj*, which means "room with a view." The mafraj often

Some of Sanaa's tower houses date back a thousand years, though they have been changed and added to over the centuries.

features windows that allow a good view of the surrounding scenery. Above these windows are fanlights of stained glass.

In the mafraj, family members visit with their friends and chew qat. The floor is covered with mattresses and cushions so everyone can get comfortable. The walls are often painted white and then decorated with geometric designs or lines of poetry.

Writing also adorns mosques. Often passages from the Qur'an are painted on the walls. Decorative writing, or calligraphy, on mosque walls and in manuscripts is an old art form in Yemen. It requires intense concentration. The most admired calligraphy is both beautiful and expressive, communicating to the reader the emotions contained in the text.

Beautiful calligraphy and ornate designs grace the walls of Yemeni mosques.

Some Yemeni jewelry styles date back thousands of years. Traditional jewelry such as this is worn only for a wedding or other special occasion.

Extraordinary Crafts

Another old Yemeni art form is jewelry. Traditional jewelry was made from silver. Jewish craftspeople were particularly skilled in working with silver. By 1950, most of the Jews in Yemen had moved to Israel. Before they were allowed to leave, Yemeni leaders required Jewish silversmiths to teach their skills to Arab craftspeople so knowledge of this traditional Yemeni art would not be lost.

In recent years, especially in cities, gold jewelry has become popular. Bits of coral, amber, and glass are often used to give pieces added color. Yemeni jewelry includes necklaces, earrings, finger rings, nose rings, and head ornaments. Also popular are small cases that hold written verses from the Qur'an.

Jambiyas are sometimes unsheathed in dances, but they are rarely used as weapons.

To Yemeni men, *jambiya* making is the most important traditional craft. Jambiyas are daggers with a short curved blade that men wear on the front of their body on a belt made of leather or woven cloth. The design of a jambiya often says something about the wearer. Certain designs are associated with specific tribes or regions. They can also indicate social standing. Sayyids and Qadis, for instance, wear jambiyas with decorated silver handles as symbols of their elite status. The most valued jambiyas of all have handles made from the horns of African rhinoceroses.

Long ago, Yemenis wove their own cloth. Now, most cloth is imported from other countries. Some craftspeople, however, still make cloth the old way, spinning cotton and linen thread by hand and coloring it with natural vegetable dyes.

In part because of the growing tourist industry, Yemenis are making an effort to preserve their traditional crafts. Leading the way is the National Handicrafts Training Center in Sanaa. The center provides space for craftspeople to display their wares to tourists looking to buy a beautiful souvenir. The capital is also the home the Museum of Traditional Arts and Crafts, which displays particularly well-made examples of Yemeni craftsmanship.

Zabid, a city in western Yemen, was once a center of weaving. Some men there still practice the old crafts.

The National Museum of Yemen

Reopened in 2006 after a major renovation, the National Museum of Yemen, in Sanaa, is the largest museum on the Arabian Peninsula. The museum has display space for about one-tenth of its collection of seventy-five thousand rare objects. Many date from ancient times, including a large number of artifacts from the pre-Islamic period in Arabia. Also on display is a vast collection of gold and silver Islamic coins.

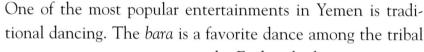

Traditional Dancing

The bara is a common dance in the highlands.

One of the most popular entertainments in Yemen is traditional dancing. The *bara* is a favorite dance among the tribal people. Each tribe has its own way of dancing the bara. In public, only men dance the bara.

Generally, bara dancers form a U-shape, with the dance leader in the center. As a drum beats, he determines the dance steps and the others follow. The steps can be very complicated and frenzied. In a standard part of the bara, the dancers wave their jambiyas in the air. They have to be careful not to accidentally nick their fellow performers.

The *l'ub* is a gentler dance that is especially popular in the highlands. People dance the l'ub in pairs, often to love songs. In public, l'ub partners are always of the same gender.

Music and Song

Music is also an important part of everyday life in Yemen. At all hours of the day, music can be heard coming from homes and storefronts. Women often listen to the radio while cooking and doing other household chores.

The Yemenis' musical traditions vary from region to region. Similarly, their traditional songs deal with a wide variety of subjects. Some recount romances, others celebrate religion, and still others explore political issues. Several Yemeni singers have begun recording traditional music. A few, including Badavi Zubayr and Salim Balfaqih, have fans throughout the Arabian Peninsula.

One of most popular instruments among urban Yemenis is the *oud*. The oud is a short lute that resembles a guitar. It produces a calming sound, although along the Tihamah coastal plain, it is played in a more spirited style, showing the influence of African and Indian music in this area. The *mizmar*, a type of windpipe, and the *simsimiya*, a lyre with five strings, are also common in Yemeni music.

The oud is shaped like a pear. It usually has eleven strings.

A Nation of Poets

As much as Yemenis love song and dance, their most treasured form of expression is poetry. Their poetic tradition spans thousands of years. Even before they had a written language, the Yemenis' ancestors memorized poems and recited them, passing them along by word of mouth from region to region and generation to generation.

Talented poets are highly regarded in Yemeni society. Some have used their art to communicate controversial ideas.

Zayd Muti Dammaj

Zayd Muti Dammaj (1943–2000) is the most famous Yemeni novelist of the twentieth century. Born in the city of Ibb, Dammaj was the son of a sheik who supported a revolt against the imams who ruled northern Yemen. Dammaj's most famous work is *Al-Raheena* (*The Hostage*). Set in the 1940s, it tells the story of a boy taken hostage by a local governor to ensure the political loyalty of the boy's father. The governor puts the boy to work at his palace. As the boy struggles with his captivity, the novel becomes a comment on the isolation the imams forced on the Yemeni people. *Al-Raheena* is one of the few Yemeni novels to reach an international audience. It has been translated into English, French, Spanish, German, Russian, and Hindi.

For instance, the work of Muhammad Mahmoud al-Zubayri helped gather support for the revolt against the imam rulers of northern Yemen in the 1960s. Another noted poet, Abdullah al-Baradduni, advocated women's rights and democratic ideals.

In Yemen, poetry is not always serious business. Making up poems is also a popular form of entertainment. At get-togethers, people will often amuse their friends by composing a poem on the spot. And at wedding celebrations, men will often challenge one another to see who can come up with the cleverest wordplay.

A Poet for Peace

"Other countries fight terrorism with guns and bombs, but in Yemen we use poetry," explains Amin al-Mashreqi. Yemen's most popular tribal poet, Mashreqi devotes himself to spreading a message of peace by traveling to remote areas and reciting his verses denouncing the terrorist acts of Islamic extremists.

Mashreqi began his mission in 2003, at the suggestion of Faris Sanabani, the editor of the *Yemen Observer* newspaper and a friend of President Ali Abdullah Saleh. Historically, the Yemeni people have had great respect for poets. Sanabani believed that many Yemenis would take to heart the words of a highly regarded poet like Mashreqi.

In his poetry, Mashreqi appeals to the Yemenis' pride in their country to persuade them to reject terrorism. One verse states:

O men of arms, why do you love injustice?
You must live in law and order.
Get up, wake up, or be forever regretful.
Don't be infamous among the nations.

For Mashreqi, using a traditional art form seems an ideal way to combat a modern problem. He explains, "If poetry contains the right ideas and is used in the right context, then people will respond to it because this is the heart of their culture."

In Yemen, any flat space might be used as a soccer field.

Playing Sports

Like many people, Yemenis enjoy sports. Soccer is by far the most popular sport. In big cities and rural villages, boys gather to play. National soccer matches are held at a sports arena in Sanaa.

A more traditional sport is camel racing. Most races are held in the desert areas of far eastern Yemen. Tribesmen there take pride in breeding camels that can run extremely fast. Selling a speedy camel can earn a breeder a small fortune.

Camels normally walk at about 3 miles (5 km) per hour. Racing camels can reach speeds of 20 miles (35 km) per hour.

Since unification, a handful of Yemeni athletes have taken part in the Olympic Games. They include runner Saeed al-Adhreai, swimmer Muhammad Saad, and tae kwon do champion Akram Abdullah. Yemen has yet to win a medal.

"Prince Naseem"

Flamboyant British boxing champion Naseem Salom Ali Hamed was not born in Yemen and he did not grow up there, but Yemenis consider him a national hero. He has been featured on a Yemeni postage stamp and was honored by Yemen's president, Ali Abdullah Saleh.

The son of Yemeni immigrants, Hamed was born in Sheffield, England, on February 12, 1974. He first picked up a boxing glove when he was only seven. From the start, his talent was obvious. He moved quickly and developed a fast and powerful left-hand punch.

Hamed became a professional boxer at age eighteen. Fighting as a featherweight, he took his first world title three years later. Hamed became known as much for his dramatic ring entrances as for his fighting. Calling himself "Prince Naseem," he was once carried into the ring on a throne. At other times, he paraded into the arena like a fashion model on a catwalk and came down from the roof in a specially built elevator.

Hamed had won thirty-five professional fights in a row when he stepped into the ring to fight Mexico's Marco Antonio Barrera in 2001. In an upset, Barrera was ruled the winner, ending Hamed's winning streak. In 2002, Hamed won one final fight. He has not returned to the ring since.

Television and Newspapers

Armchair athletes in Yemen can enjoy sports by watching them on television. Other popular TV programs include cartoons, soap operas, and comedies, many of which are produced in other Arab countries, such as Egypt and Syria. Yemen has two TV networks, which are both run by the government. In parts of Yemen, viewers can receive broadcasts from TV stations in the neighboring countries of Oman and Saudi Arabia.

In cities, watching TV is usually a family affair. Everyone in the household gathers together to enjoy their favorite shows. In villages, where fewer people have TV sets, friends and neighbors often get together in big groups to watch.

About half of Yemenis cannot read. For them, TV is the primary source of news. Yemenis who can read rely on a wide variety of newspapers, including four dailies. The government keeps tight control over the press and frequently harasses journalists and newspapers that publish stories that cast the government in a bad light. Even so, for an Arab country, Yemen has a relatively free press. This allows Yemenis to gain a better understanding of what is happening in their country and in the world beyond.

Children in Sanaa gather around televisions to play video games.

Everyday Life

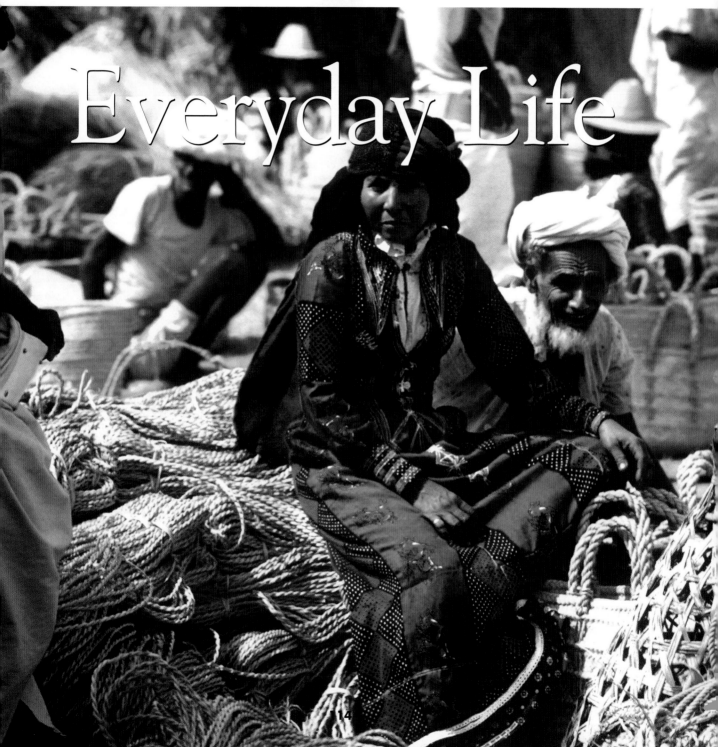

F OR THE PEOPLE OF YEMEN, THERE IS ALWAYS TIME FOR socializing. In the villages, Yemenis live close to one another. As they go about their daily work, neighbors regularly take a break to talk with one another. They might discuss what their families are up to, exchange local news, or spread a bit of the latest village gossip.

In the cities, the pace of life is faster, and people often find themselves surrounded by strangers. Still, urban Yemenis manage to carve out moments for brief social interactions throughout the day. They may chat with friends at a mosque after morning prayers or exchange small talk with vendors

Opposite: **Goods are piled high at a market in Yemen.**

Few women are seen on the streets of Yemen's cities.

at an open-air market. Even at business meetings, Yemenis always fit in a little personal conversation. As a show of courtesy, colleagues will ask each other about their friends and families before getting down to work.

Chewing Qat

Throughout Yemen, men leave work for hours during the afternoon. They spend this break at get-togethers where they enjoy conversation with friends while indulging in the Yemeni national pastime—chewing qat.

Chomping on the leaves of the qat bush releases a stimulant. The effect is sometimes compared to consuming a large

Chewing qat is central to Yemeni culture. The average Yemeni spends more money on qat than on food.

amount of caffeine. Yemenis claim that qat clears the mind and helps them make decisions. At qat parties, Yemeni men sometimes talk business and make deals with one another. But most of time, chewing qat is entirely social.

Sometimes, men chewing qat will joke with one another and exchange witty insults. Other times, they will become absorbed in serious conversation about politics or religion. As the hours pass, they may take turns reciting poetry or, on special occasions, sing and dance.

Men's qat parties often last as long as four hours. They are held at home, sometimes in a special room. Each morning, friends make plans for who will host that day's party. Because qat loses its potency soon after it is picked, part of the morning is also devoted to buying fresh leaves. The best quality qat is expensive. A day's dose can cost the equivalent of US$50. Most people, though, can only afford lower-quality qat, priced at about US$3. But even this is a fair amount of money to average Yemenis. Some people spend half their daily income on qat.

Some women have afternoon parties called *tafritah* circles. Guests dress up and gather at a friend's house. There, they drink glasses of sweet tea and snack on raisins and nuts. As they relax and talk, older women often tell stories. Mothers sometimes bring their daughters, who are expected be on their best behavior.

Some women chew qat at these gatherings. Qat is now so popular that an estimated 80 percent of adult men and women in Yemen chew it on a regular basis.

Saltah

Yemeni cooks are famous for *saltah*. Especially popular in Sanaa, saltah is a hearty, spicy stew. It is often made with lentils, chickpeas, potatoes, and chunks of chicken, lamb, and beef. A sauce called *hilbah*, which means "fenugreek," is spooned on top. Fenugreek is an herb with a slightly bitter taste, and hilbah is soaked fenugreek with spices added. The mixture is whipped into a froth.

Saltah is served piping hot. It is eaten by dipping flat bread into it. Many Yemenis consider tasty and filling saltah the perfect lunch.

Mealtime

Meals are another time for socializing, in this case with family members. Instead of gathering around a table, diners sit on the floor, which is covered with a colorful plastic cloth or woven mat. Yemenis usually do not use utensils. Instead, they eat from shared bowls, using a piece of bread or their fingers to take what they want.

The cuisine of Yemen varies from region to region because different foods are available in different areas. But generally, the Yemeni diet is built around grains, such as sorghum and millet, and locally grown fruits and vegetables.

Yemenis usually have a light breakfast, consisting of porridge or perhaps an egg or beans with bread. Dinner is also a small meal, often featuring bread and leftovers. For most Yemenis, the big meal of the day is lunch. It is likely to include a stew or soup and plenty of vegetable dishes. Bread is often served with a dipping sauce, such as *fuul*, a spicy mixture of beans, tomatoes, and onions.

Meat and Bread

Meat is expensive, so only the wealthy eat it often. Most families might enjoy mutton or beef on special occasions or when a guest is visiting. In coastal areas, freshly caught fish is a common part of the midday meal. Yemenis never eat pork because Islamic law forbids it.

Yemenis eat bread with every meal. There are more than forty different kinds made in Yemen. At home, women cook *khubz tawwa*, a type of fried bread. In shops, they often buy large loafs of *ruti*. For special meals, they might serve *lahuh*, a pancake made from sorghum. And for a treat, Yemenis enjoy *bint al-sahn*, a dessert of sweet bread topped with honey and butter.

Traditionally, Yemenis pick up food with bread or their fingers. Spoons are becoming more common, however.

Yemenis are proud of the delicious honey produced in the Hadhramaut region. They often give jars of it to friends as gifts. Some Yemenis swear by honey as a cure for stomachaches and sore throats.

Beverages

After a meal, Yemenis often relax together over a hot beverage. The most popular is tea. Sweet tea, called *shay*, is a particular favorite, especially in the city of Aden. The people there make tea by first adding sugar to a pot of water. They then bring the water to a boil and drop in tea leaves and spices, such as cardamom. The tea is served in small glasses. Oftentimes, Yemenis add milk to their tea.

Many Yemenis mix their tea with milk. Some also add cardamom and other spices.

Yemenis also enjoy coffee, which is hardly surprising given that Yemen produces some of the best coffee beans in the world. Yemeni beans are small and hard. They produce a rich brew with a creamy texture and an almost chocolaty taste. Yemenis often flavor their coffee with ginger.

Nonalcoholic beer is also widely consumed in Yemen. Muslim Yemenis do not drink alcohol because their religion prohibits it. Alcohol is available in some hotels and restaurants, especially those that cater to Western tourists.

Marriage Customs

In Yemen, men and women rarely socialize with one another. As a result, most young people do not choose their own husband or wife. Instead, they rely on relatives to select a spouse for them.

A courtship begins when a young man's parents agree on a possible bride. They talk about the woman with their son. If he is interested, he and his father visit the woman's father. The woman's father will then discuss the proposal with his daughter. If everyone agrees to the marriage, the groom and his father offer gifts and money to the bride's family. The young man and young woman are then officially engaged.

Yemeni weddings are lavish affairs that often go on for days. At the ceremony, a Qadi recites from the Qur'an. A big feast follows, during which the groom's friends sing and dance. To celebrate the new couple, women throughout the neighborhood climb to the rooftops and sing of their happiness.

Paying Respect

Yemenis are well known for their hospitality. They are always pleased to welcome guests into their homes. By custom, hosts offer guests the best of everything they have, from food to drink to entertainment. Guests have an obligation to cheerfully accept whatever they are offered. To turn down a meal from a host would be regarded as an incredible insult.

Yemenis also show great respect to the elderly. Most households contain many people and several generations. Everyone in the family is expected to obey the wishes of the oldest members. Older people are considered wise and therefore are often asked to settle disputes.

There are relatively few elderly people in Yemen, however. Life expectancy is low, only about sixty years of age, largely because of inadequate health care. In some parts of the country, there are few doctors. Hospital space is so limited that women almost always give birth at home with the help of female family members. Without access to modern medicine, many Yemenis rely on traditional herbal remedies. Some wear charms and amulets that ward off evil forces that they believe could make them sick.

Yemen has a shortage of teachers, which limits the number of children who can get an education. By law, all children between six and fifteen are supposed to be in school. But in fact, just 57 percent actually are. Boys are far more likely to go to school than girls.

Many uneducated children live in rural areas. In some cases, they don't go to school because they have no way to get there. In others, their families need them to stay at home and work. For farm families, making a living is extremely hard. They need the labor of every family member, no matter how young or small, if they hope to survive.

Boys are far more likely to be educated in Yemen than girls. About 70 percent of men can read and write, while only 30 percent of women can.

In all Yemeni families, parents teach their children the roles they will adopt as adults. Girls are taught how to do household chores and look after younger children. Boys learn how to conduct business and operate and repair machinery. Both are given opportunities to play, but even then, their gender dictates what they are allowed to do. Boys are likely to be out and about, playing board games, marbles, or cards outside in the marketplace. Girls are expected to stay near home, playing with dolls or singing and dancing with their friends.

Early on, Yemeni children discover that men and women live in different spheres. Even as adults, most women spend most of their time in their homes. They rarely venture far from the neighborhood. Women are charged with taking care of the house and the children. Men do just about everything that requires contact with the public, including shopping for food and household goods at open-air markets. Increasingly, Yemeni women are obtaining formal educations and working outside the home, but most still live according to the traditional gender roles.

Clothing

The Qur'an instructs Muslims to dress modestly. This can be interpreted in many ways. In Yemen, many women wear face veils when they are around men outside their family. Some Yemeni women wear a *sharshaf*, a loose black robe that covers their entire body, including their head.

For women and for men, clothing styles differ from region to region. Women in the deserts of eastern Yemen favor black

robes, while those in the Tihamah like bright colors. The women of the Wadi Hadhramaut are known for their tall palm hats. In rural areas, women wear woolen shawls when traveling outside their village. In the cities, women and men are apt to combine Western clothing, like suits and blazers, with Yemeni garments.

Some women in Yemen wear a veil that leaves only a gap for their eyes.

Yemeni women decorate their skin on special occasions.

In Yemen, clothes say a great deal about where people are from and their status in society. For instance, the traditional clothing of tribal men includes a *futa* (a kind of wraparound skirt), a turban, and a jambiya (dagger) worn on a belt. Men signal their tribal membership by the way they tie their turbans. The design of their jambiya similarly indicates their social rank.

For certain religious festivals, women decorate their hands and feet. These designs may be made with henna, a plant dye, or with kohl, a black cosmetic. Some urban women hire a body painter for the evening before their wedding day. Using a needle or a toothpick, the painter creates beautiful patterns with henna on the woman's hands, arms, feet, and legs. Brides also adorn themselves with their finest silver jewelry.

Celebrating Yemen

Throughout the year, the Yemeni people come together for a number of national celebrations. For instance, on May 1 they celebrate the Yemeni worker with Labor Day festivities.

Yemenis also observe several holidays that remind them of pivotal days in their history. There are two Revolution Day celebrations. On September 26, Revolution Day honors the 1962 military-led uprising that ended the imams' rule in northern Yemen. On October 14, Revolution Day commemorates the day in 1967, when the National Liberation Front began its successful revolution, which eventually drove the British out of southern Yemen. Another holiday that grew out of southern Yemen's history is Independence Day, which is celebrated on November 30. It marks the anniversary of the establishment of the People's Democratic Republic of Yemen in 1970.

Yemeni Holidays	
Labor Day	May 1
Day of National Unity	May 22
Revolution Day	September 26
Revolution Day	October 14
Independence Day	November 30

The most important national holiday in Yemen is the Day of National Unity. It celebrates the most important event in modern Yemeni history—the creation of the unified Republic of Yemen on May 22, 1990. Every May 22, Yemenis across the nation take the day off. They hold dances, watch soccer matches, and enjoy camel races. Hundreds of thousands crowd into the streets to march in parades. Waving Yemen's flag and singing the national anthem, together they express their love for their young country and their hopes for a prosperous future for all Yemeni people.

Timeline

Yemeni History		World History	
		2500 B.C.	Egyptians build the pyramids and the Sphinx in Giza.
The Kingdom of Saba emerges in southern Arabia.	ca. 1000 B.C.		
		563 B.C.	The Buddha is born in India.
The Himyarites become the dominant force in southern Arabia.	ca. A.D. 300	A.D. 313	The Roman emperor Constantine legalizes Christianity.
		610	The Prophet Muhammad begins preaching a new religion called Islam.
The Persian governor of southern Arabia converts to Islam.	628		
The Zaydis, a Shi'i sect, take over northern Yemen.	ca. 890		
		1054	The Eastern (Orthodox) and Western (Roman Catholic) Churches break apart.
		1095	The Crusades begin.
		1215	King John seals the Magna Carta.
		1300s	The Renaissance begins in Italy.
		1347	The plague sweeps through Europe.
		1453	Ottoman Turks capture Constantinople, conquering the Byzantine Empire.
		1492	Columbus arrives in North America.
The Ottoman Empire conquers Aden, Taizz, and Sanaa.	1530s–1540s	1500s	Reformers break away from the Catholic Church, and Protestantism is born.
The Zaydis drive the Ottoman Turks from the region.	1636		
		1776	The Declaration of Independence is signed.
		1789	The French Revolution begins.
The British navy seizes Aden.	1839		

The Ottoman Turks regain control of northern Yemen.	1849	1865	The American Civil War ends.
		1879	The first practical light bulb is invented.
The British and the Turks established a border between the areas they control in Yemen.	1905		
		1914	World War I begins.
		1917	The Bolshevik Revolution brings communism to Russia.
Turkish occupation of North Yemen ends.	1920		
		1929	A worldwide economic depression begins.
		1939	World War II begins.
		1945	World War II ends.
Yahya bin Muhammad Hamid al-Din is assassinated by a rebel group.	1948		
		1957	The Vietnam War begins.
Civil war breaks out in northern Yemen after a military coup establishing the Yemen Arab Repbublic.	1962		
British troops leave Aden and the surrounding area; the People's Republic of South Yemen is established.	1967		
		1969	Humans land on the Moon.
The republicans win the civil war in the Yemen Arab Republic; the People's Republic of South Yemen changes its name to the People's Democratic Republic of Yemen.	1970		
		1975	The Vietnam War ends.
Ali Abdullah Saleh becomes president of the Yemen Arab Republic.	1978		
The Yemen Arab Republic and the People's Democratic Republic of Yemen unite to form the Republic of Yemen.	1990	1989	The Berlin Wall is torn down as communism crumbles in Eastern Europe.
		1991	The Soviet Union breaks into separate states.
Civil war breaks out.	1994		
Saleh is elected president in Yemen's first popular presidential election.	1999		
Al-Qaeda terrorists bomb the USS *Cole* anchored at Aden, killing 17 Americans.	2000	2001	Terrorists attack the World Trade Center in New York City and the Pentagon in Washington, D.C.
President Saleh is reelected to a seven-year term.	2006		

Fast Facts

Official name: Republic of Yemen

Capital: Sanaa

Official language: Arabic

Sanaa

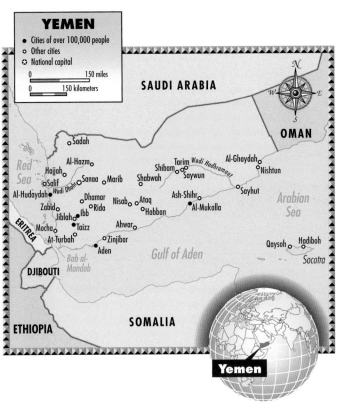

Yemen's flag

Desert rose

Official religion:	Islam
Year of founding:	1990
National anthem:	"United Republic"
Government:	Republic
Chief of state:	President
Head of government:	Prime minister
Area:	203,850 square miles (527,968 sq km)
Latitude and longitude of geographic center:	15°00' N, 48°00' E
Bordering countries:	Oman and Saudi Arabia
Highest elevation:	12,336 feet (3,760 m), at Jabal an-Nabi Shu'ayb
Lowest elevation:	Sea level, along the coast
Highest average temperature:	June, 80°F (27°C)
Lowest average temperature:	January, 57°F (14°C)
Highest annual rainfall:	In the highlands, 8 to 30 inches (20 to 76 cm)
Lowest annual rainfall:	Along the coast, 3 to 9 inches (7 to 22 cm)
National population (2006 est.):	21,456,458

Dar al-Hajar

Currency

Population of largest cities (2005 est.):

Sanaa	1,653,300
Aden	510,400
Taizz	406,900
Al-Hudaydah	382,400
Al-Mukalla	156,800

Famous landmarks:
- ▶ *Dar al-Hajar*, Wadi Dhahr
- ▶ *Great Mosque of Sanaa*, Sanaa
- ▶ *National Museum of Yemen*, Sanaa
- ▶ *Great Dam of Marib*, Marib
- ▶ *Temple of Bilqis*, Marib
- ▶ *Queen Awra Mosque*, Jiblah

Industry: Oil production is Yemen's most lucrative industry. In 2005, the oil industry accounted for 70 percent of the Yemeni government's total revenues. Most Yemenis work in agriculture. The major products include coffee and sorghum. Yemen's manufacturing industry is growing. Products manufactured in Yemen include processed foods and building materials. Yemen also has a growing tourism industry.

Currency: Yemen's basic unit of currency is the rial. In 2007, 1 U.S. dollar was worth about 198 rials.

System of weights and measures: Metric system

Literacy rate: 50%

Arabic words and phrases:

Al salaam alaykum.	Hello.
Ma'al salaama.	Good-bye.
Tisbah ala-kher (to a man); *tisbihin ala-kher* (to a woman).	Good night.

Schoolchildren

Ali Abdullah Saleh

Fursa sa'ida.	Pleased to meet you.
Kayf al-hal?	How are you?
Baraka Allah beek.	Thank you.
Afwan.	You're welcome.
Lau samaht (to a man);	
lau samahti (to a woman).	Excuse me.
Kam as-sa'a?	What time is it?
Bhismak? (to a man);	
bismish? (to a woman)	What is your name?
Ismi . . .	My name is . . .

Famous People:

Arwa (1048–1138)
Queen of the Sulayhid dynasty

Abdullah al-Baradduni (1929–1999)
Poet

Zayd Muti Dammaj (1943–2000)
Novelist

Yahya bin Muhammad Hamid al-Din (1895–1962)
Imam and political leader

Abu Muhammad al-Hasan ibn (ca. 893–945)
Ahmad al-Hamdani
Poet, geographer, and historian

Ali Abdullah Saleh (1942–)
President

Queen of Sheba (ca. 900s B.C.)
Ruler of the ancient Sabean kingdom

Muhammad Mahmoud al-Zubayri (1919–1965)
Poet and reformer

To Find Out More

Books

- Alkouatli, Claire. *Islam*. Tarrytown, NY: Marshall Cavendish, 2007.

- Hestler, Anna. *Yemen*. Tarrytown, NY: Marshall Cavendish, 1999.

- Kort, Michael. *The Handbook of the Middle East*. Brookfield, CT: Twenty-first Century Books, 2002.

- Marcovitz, Hal. *Yemen*. Philadelphia: Mason Crest Publishers, 2004.

- Romano, Amy. *A Historical Atlas of Yemen*. New York: Rosen Publishing Group, 2004.

- Weber, Sandra. *Yemen*. Philadelphia: Chelsea House Publishers, 2003.

Web Sites

- **The Republic of Yemen**
  www.yemen.gov.ye/egov/egov-english/index.html
  To find information about Yemen's government, history, and culture.

▶ **The World Factbook**
https://www.cia.gov/cia/publications/
factbook/geos/ym.html
*For an array of current statistics about
Yemen and its people.*

▶ **Yemen Times**
www.yementimes.com
*For news and feature articles from
Yemen's weekly English-language
newspaper.*

Organizations and Embassies

▶ **Embassy of the Republic of Yemen**
2319 Wyoming Avenue, NW
Washington, DC 20008
202-965-4760
www.yemenembassy.org

▶ **Embassy of the Republic of Yemen in Canada**
54 Chamberlain Avenue
Ottawa, Ontario
Canada K1S 1V9
613-729-6627
www.yemenincanada.ca

Index

Page numbers in *italics* indicate illustrations.

Meet the Author

AGRADUATE OF SWARTHMORE COLLEGE, LIZ SONNEBORN lives in Brooklyn, New York. She has written more than fifty nonfiction books for children and adults on a wide variety of subjects. Her books include *The American West*, *A to Z of American Indian Women*, *The Ancient Kushites*, *The Vietnamese Americans*, and *Guglielmo Marconi*.

Tackling Yemen was something new for Sonneborn. She had never before written a book about a Middle Eastern country. The project was a welcome challenge, though, because she has a personal interest in Yemen. Her neighborhood in Brooklyn is near a community of Yemeni immigrants. According to Sonneborn, "Researching and writing this book was a wonderful opportunity to get a better understanding of my neighbors, their heritage, and their native land." She was especially pleased to be able to identify the ceramic miniatures found in Yemeni storefronts as models of the Dar al-Hajar palace, one of the most famous buildings in Yemen.

Sonneborn began her research on Yemen as she often does on an unfamiliar topic—reading the best general overviews she could find on the subject. Paul Dresch's *History of Modern Yemen* was particularly helpful. After putting together a rough outline for the book, she then began rooting out articles and other writings on more specific subjects she needed to understand better. In this case, Web sites were the best source of information, especially about elements of Yemeni life and society that are changing rapidly. Of the dozens of Web sites she explored, the most interesting and useful was that of the *Yemen Times* (www.yementimes.com), a Yemeni newspaper written in English. Its articles, particularly its features on everyday life, gave the author a sense of how Yemenis themselves view their culture and their country.

Photo Credits